# DR. HERB'S SOLUTIONS
## to the Root Causes of
# STRESS

# *Dr. Herb's Solutions*
## to the Root Causes of
# STRESS

DR. HERBERT I. SCHUCK, N.D., MSc

*Dr. Herb's Solutions to the Root Causes of Stress*
Copyright © 2018 by Dr. Herbert Schuck. All rights reserved.

No part of this publication may be reproduced, stored in a retrieval system or transmitted in any way by any means, electronic, mechanical, photocopy, recording or otherwise without the prior permission of the author except as provided by USA copyright law.

The opinions expressed by the author are not necessarily those of URLink Print and Media.

1603 Capitol Ave., Suite 310 Cheyenne, Wyoming USA 82001
1-888-980-6523 | admin@urlinkpublishing.com

URLink Print and Media is committed to excellence in the publishing industry.

Book design copyright © 2018 by URLink Print and Media. All rights reserved.

Published in the United States of America
ISBN 978-1-64367-103-1 (Paperback)
ISBN 978-1-64367-102-4 (Digital)

Non-Fiction
27.10.18

# Dedication

*This book is dedicated
to my family my friends
and my patients*

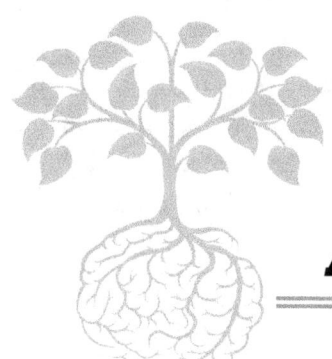

# Acknowledgments

Many thanks to Dr. J.R. Millenson, *Mind Matters* for the use of *Work Stress* and *Life Events Stress* charts and to Thomas H. Holmes, M.D., Dept. of Psychiatry and Behavioral Sciences, U.W. School of Medicine, Seattle, WA 98195

Thea Singer in *Stress Less* for a comprehensive review of the research

Dr. Elson Haas, *Staying Healthy with Nutrition*

Dr. David D. Clarke, *They Can't Find Anything Wrong*

Dr. Mark Percival, *Understanding Healthcare and Stress Management*

Dr. K. Pelletier, *Mind as Healer*

Pritchett and Pound, *The Stress of Organizational Change*

Dawn Grover, *Meditation for Busy People*

Drs. Bloomfield and Cooper, *The Power of 5*

Dr. Christine Dargon, PhD., *Anxiety in Children and Adolescents*

Ms. Florie Freshman for the free-form book illustrations DiagnosTechs for "Adrenal Stress Seminars" and definitive stages of stress

Ms. Jenae Williams for GPL-Tox information

*Dr. Herb's Solutions to the Root Causes of Stress*

Tracy F. Rysavy of Green America for GMO comments and illustrations

## DR. HERBERT I. SCHUCK

Mr. Will Terry for his unique illustration on "American Fast Food Cravings" in Psychology Today, 1993

Most importantly, I wish to commend Ari Guth, Jacob and Joseph Rosenstock of Guth-Rosenstock Art, guthrart@aol.com for their great cover and book design, two illustrations, interior layout, editing of the manuscript and help in the publication process.

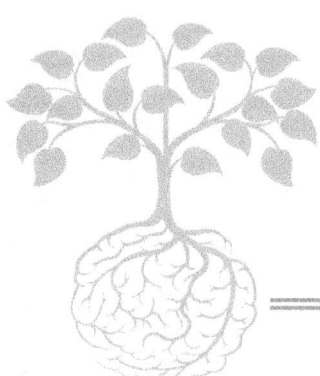

# Contents

Acknowledgments .................................................................. vii

Introduction ............................................................................. xi

Chapter 1: Definition of Stress .................................................. 1

Chapter 2: Workplace Stressors ................................................. 5
    *Measuring Your Stress At Work* ................................................ 7
    *Schedule Of Recent Life Events* ............................................... 10
    *Stress Evaluation Form* ........................................................ 13

Chapter 3: Illnesses Related To Stress ..................................... 15
    *Emotions, Stress and Physiology* ............................................ 16
    *The Three Parts of the Brain* ................................................. 18

Chapter 4: Chronic Stress, Physiology and Solutions ................ 23

Chapter 5: Parental and Child Relationships ........................... 37
    *Children and Toxic Stress* ..................................................... 38

Chapter 6: Stress and Telomeres .............................................. 43

Chapter 7: Food Choices, the GI Tract and Testing ................. 49
    *Gluten, Celiac Disease and Testing* ....................................... 50
    *Irritable Bowel Disease (IBD), IBS and SIBO* ........................ 55

*Food Allergies and Food Intolerance* .................................................. *60*
*Allergies and GMOs* ............................................................. *66*
*Peanuts update* .................................................................. *73*
*Specific Pollutants* ............................................................... *76*
*Heavy Metal Toxicity—New Information* ........................... *77*
*Regenerative Agriculture* ...................................................... *79*

Chapter 8: Societal Stress ..................................................... 85
    *Suicides* ........................................................................... *86*

Chapter 9: Lifestyle Changes.................................................. 89
    *New Choices Wanted For Retirees* ...................................... *89*

Chapter 10: Meditation, Cognitive Behavioral
Therapy and Mindfulness ....................................................... 93

Chapter 11: Creative Modalities—Art, Music ........................ 99

Conclusion ............................................................................. 103

Appendix A ............................................................................ 105

Appendix B ............................................................................ 107

References .............................................................................. 111

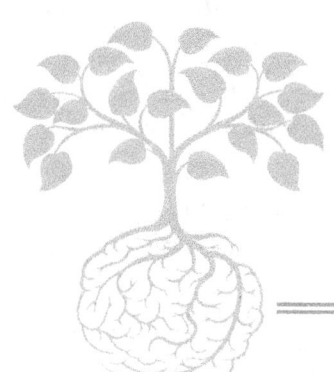

# Introduction

It would seem that leaving the year 2016 without mentioning some insights into what has been a turbulent year would border on negligence. In Judaic Biblical terms, we all welcome the coming of Messiah to bring peace in the world. What precedes this, however is the Battle of Gog and Magog where society will self-destruct and survivors will build a new civilization of peaceful coexistence.

The years 2014 to 2016 have been the most turbulent on a physical level: earthquakes in Japan and Asia, tsunamis in the Philippines, flooding in Asia, tornadoes and drought in the Midwest and other parts of the US, volcanic eruptions in Italy and South America, and rising sea levels, especially in coastal areas of the US—at least 11 inches or more in New York and Boston, Charleston, Atlantic City, Norfolk, and Galveston, Texas. Fossil fuel emissions and the heat-trapping of greenhouse gases, warming of the oceans with melting of glaciers and ice sheets also drive sea creatures and fish to seek cooler waters instead of traditional habitats. It can also disrupt reproduction from toxic sewage and "plastics" dumping. Rio De Janeiro, Brazil, still dumps raw sewage into Guanabara Bay where the 2016 Olympics were held.

On a mental/emotional level, stress in our society continues to rise with increased robotic production and fewer workers being pressured to increase productivity. Continuing mergers and cost-cutting further reduces workers. "Made in the USA" used to be a mark of pride and quality, but the auto industry, for example, has had record recalls in the past several years.

On a humanistic level, personal violence has reached unprecedented levels with school, home, and workplace killings in the US and overseas—slaughter of families in Nigeria, Zimbabwe, Darfur, and other areas of South Africa, Asia, Syria (over 400,000), and in Egypt (Coptic Christians).

There has been unrest and public riots in China, Russia, Turkey, and other countries. In the US, it is particularly troubling that despite shootings and pleading of concerned parties, stricter gun control is consistently blocked by the National Rifle Association (NRA).

One of the primary causes of violence is mental illness in the young, particularly with teenagers who go undiagnosed and either turn their weapons on their peers and then commit suicide or survive to end up in prison. Mental illness has many facets—harassment or abuse by peers for being "different," which can result in suicide. In sports, there are more suicides again from harassment or stress created by peers or undiagnosed, untreated depression.

In the Armed Services, screening for mental illness should be part of the complete physical exam. Discharged servicemen and women, especially those who have been in battle should be routinely offered counseling and be screened for suicidal ideation or post-traumatic stress disorder (PTSD). Families of service personnel should be alerted for signs in returning spouses of depression, insomnia or suicidal thoughts with lack of employment.

A final disturbing note from a father whose life was spared only by the fact that he was at work, not at home, because his 40 year old son killed the rest of the family including a 6-month old baby. The father had been trying for 20 years to get his schizophrenic son committed to mental hospitals but he was routinely released to live at home.

Lastly, a headline of an ex-combat veteran back from Afghanistan who killed innocent bystanders in a drug house over the narcotic, oxycodone/APAP. The vet was diagnosed as bipolar and suffered from post-traumatic stress disorder (PTSD). Mental health issues such as these appear to be more prominent when there is increased societal stress or personal undiagnosed stress left untreated.

## Your dis - stress checklist

### Are you experiencing...

| | Yes | No |
|---|---|---|
| Pounding heart | | |
| Elevated blood pressure | | |
| Sweating | | |
| Headache | | |
| Sleep disturbances | | |
| Skin rashes | | |
| Trembling or tics | | |
| Irritability and impatience | | |
| Depression | | |
| Fearfulness | | |
| Low self - esteem | | |
| Envy | | |
| Loss of interest in your job | | |
| Eating too much or too little | | |
| Drinking more alcohol | | |
| Pacing or restlessness | | |
| Increased smoking | | |
| Teeth grinding, nail biting, other nervous behaviors | | |
| Aggressive driving | | |
| Forgetfulness | | |
| Mind racing or going blank | | |
| Indecisiveness | | |
| Resistance to change | | |
| Diminished sense of humor | | |
| Declining productivity | | |

**Interpreting your responses:** If you answered "Yes" to more than half of these statements, you may be suffering from physical, emotional, behavioral and mental manifestations of di-stress.

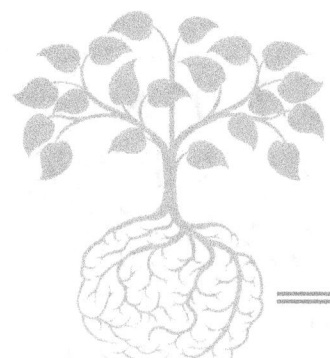

# Chapter 1

## Definition of Stress

Stress is defined as demand on physical or mental energy or the distress (suffering) caused by stress. It is derived from French, *estresse*, meaning narrowness or oppression— a limiting of power. Strain, tension and burden are synonymous with *estresse*.

Stress is the most debilitating when perceived as "negative stress" or a threat to increasing demands. This sets off the adrenal/hypothalamic axis of cortisol/adrenaline excess which can contract cardiac muscle fibers, weakening them and raising cholesterol, leading to hardening of the arteries. This mismanaged "negative stress" affects all body systems—immune, heart, nervous system, memory and thought. It also affects physical coordination and metabolic rate, increases cholesterol, blood pressure and uric acid levels. It also promotes susceptibility to disease. There is a link to greater abdominal body fat and destruction of brain cells, promoting premature aging and triggering emotional lability.

Understanding the stress response did not take place until the Great American Depression. In 1935, Walter Cannon described the extraordinary ability of the body to respond to stress, or "accidents of existence" (Cannon, 1935).

DR. HERBERT I. SCHUCK

© Guth-Rosenstock Art 2017, all rights reserved

He labeled the stressed-induced increases in cardiac output as "fight or flight" and he recognized adrenal hormones in this response as early as 1924.

In 1936, Hans Selye, M.D., labeled this response as the "general adaptation syndrome" (GAS). In 1956, he published *The Stress of Life*, whereby he describes how humans respond to stress through neuroendocrine and behavioral-emotional components resulting in the GAS syndrome. Depending on the type of stressor, whether it may be "attacking you in the woods," or "the boss at work," the response is similar or acute depending on the individual's perception. Initially, we compensate and calm down. In a continued or chronic situation, where stress is ongoing, either at home or at work, we again compensate, i.e., the body rebounds, but hormonally the body resets internally at a higher level—with increased blood pressure or higher blood sugar levels which in turn can inhibit certain components of immune function. With ongoing stress or *distress*, coping moves from an *overcompensated* to a *decompensated* state. At the latter stage, we can lose sleep and become more fatigued and depressed. Since stress is cumulative, it becomes more urgent to deal with the "root causes" from both a psychological as well as a physical perspective and see a practitioner who is experienced in this field.

Mark Percival, D.C., N.D. in his *Health Coach Program* denotes specific "environmental" stressors that need to be dealt with:

- *Mental/Emotional stressors:* "Every thought we think has an impact on every cell in our body."
- *Chemical stressors:* Specific toxins we breathe or touch in our environment, or take in through incomplete or fast foods and drink can determine our energy or lack therof. This constitutes our data bank for daily labors.
- *Physical/Structural stressors:* Gravity as much as injuries can influence our posture, bone structure and the effort it takes us to be functional.

- *Electromagnetic stressors:* Our bodies are constantly in a state of flux or flow, i.e., electrical, as measured by EEG, EKG, and electromyography. We are vulnerable to seizures and increased cancer risk from electromagnetic fields from sources such as high power lines, electrical appliances, computers and cellphones.

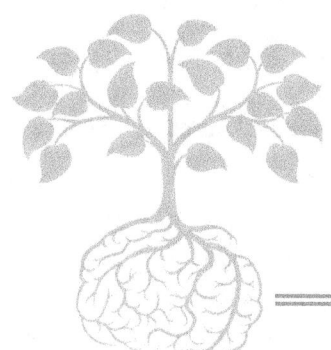

# Chapter 2

## *Workplace Stressors*

In American society of the twenty-first century, a stressful lifestyle is the norm. In particular, competition for job positions brings hundreds of applicants whether in person or on-line. Cash coffers of large corporations are full, yet they hire fewer workers due to advanced technologies. The result is using part-time help in order to avoid paying benefits. Unemployment remains high at 4.9%; up to 12% in New England, and rural Appalachia.

Viewing the population as a whole, most drug treatments for stress consist of prescription sedatives or sleeping medications that do not directly address the problem (stress) or dismiss this very important cause as being "in the head." There is a constant onslaught of drug advertising in the media which people mistakenly think will cure their stress through treating their anxiety, depression or insomnia. For example, one symptom of stress is reflux or GERD for which Proton Pump Inhibitors (PPI's) are commonly prescribed.

In the workplace, worry and anxiety can decrease productivity, affect health, drain energy, and damage relationships. Stress can aggravate existing situations or enhance negative feelings which can reduce team effectiveness. Worry becomes toxic when you feel threatened by the world and have lost the power to control your world. The simple equation illustrates the issue:

**Increased vulnerability + Decreased power = Increased worry.**

You need to recognize the difference between toxic worry that can harm you and healthy, protective worry which will help you to solve problems. *Evaluate-plan-remediate to solve problems*, i.e., identify the problem, plan a solution and take action. Wise worry can energize you to action.

Major work stressors are:

- *Changes in the workplace leading to negative stressors.*
- *An unhealthy work environment.*
- *Individual responses of anxiety or worry.*

Work environments can be overloaded with stress when staff is reduced, overtime increases, supervisors are difficult, and coworkers are negative. Negative individual responses to stress arise from fear of failure, low self-esteem, lack of trust, isolation of workers in cubicles and job burnout. Signs of distress can be physical, mental/emotional, and/or behavioral.

There are more detailed charts following to qualify your stressors: *Measuring Your Stress at Work* and the *Schedule of Recent Life Events*. The charts will reveal how to help maintain your health and prevent illness. *(Take the two following tests to determine the impact on your life and that of your family.)*

## *Measuring Your Stress At Work*

*(Please fill in to look at your stressors and how you cope with them.)*

Do you feel more stressed at work than one year ago?
- ☐ *Yes*
- ☐ *No*

When you feel stress, what physical signs do you show?
- ☐ *Headaches*
- ☐ *Stomach/Bowel problems*
- ☐ *Chest pains*
- ☐ *Frequent infections*
- ☐ *Sleep problems*
- ☐ *Weight gain or loss*
- ☐ *Loss of libido*
- ☐ *Other—Specify*

By what psychological signs do you show this stress?
- ☐ *Moodiness, irritability*
- ☐ *Tiredness*
- ☐ *Apathy*
- ☐ *Depression*
- ☐ *Anxiety*
- ☐ *Frustration*
- ☐ *Indecision*
- ☐ *Boredom*
- ☐ *Guilt feelings*
- ☐ *Poor concentration*
- ☐ *Other—Specify*

By what behavioral signs does it show?

- ☐ *Being accident-prone*
- ☐ *Alcohol abuse*
- ☐ *Drug abuse*
- ☐ *Aggressiveness*
- ☐ *Relationship problems*
- ☐ *Absenteeism*
- ☐ *Other—Specify*

How does stress in your personal life affect you at work?

- ☐ *Not at all*
- ☐ *A bit*
- ☐ *Quite a lot*
- ☐ *Very much*

How does stress at work affect your personal life?

- ☐ *Not at all*
- ☐ *A bit*
- ☐ *Quite a lot*
- ☐ *Very much*

What are the major causes of your stress?

- ☐ *Excessive workload*
- ☐ *Lack of resources*
- ☐ *Problems with colleagues*
- ☐ *Problems with management*
- ☐ *Personal difficulties*
- ☐ *Other—Specify*

## WORKPLACE STRESSORS

What facilities are provided at work to help you cope?
- ☐ *Counseling services*
- ☐ *Support groups*
- ☐ *Recreation facilities*
- ☐ *Other—Specify*

What other strategies do you use to cope with stress?
- ☐ *Relaxation/physical exercise*
- ☐ *Talking to colleagues*
- ☐ *Taking regular breaks*
- ☐ *Don't bring work home*
- ☐ *Drinking alcohol*
- ☐ *Drinking coffee or tea*
- ☐ *Taking drugs*
- ☐ *Other—specify*

How do you rate your abilities to cope with stress?
- ☐ *Poor*
- ☐ *Average*
- ☐ *Better than average*
- ☐ *Very good*

How many sick days were taken in the last year?

How many days were stress-related?

## Schedule Of Recent Life Events

*(Please note events which have occurred in the **past year** and check if applicable.)*

## PART A

☐ 1. A lot more or less trouble with the boss.
☐ 2. A major change in sleeping habits.
☐ 3. A major change in eating habits (too much or too little or different meal hours or setting)
☐ 4. A revision of personal habits (dress, manners, etc.)
☐ 5. A major change in your usual type and/or amount of recreation.
☐ 6. A major change in social activities (clubs, dancing, films, etc.)
☐ 7. A major change in religious activities.
☐ 8. A major change in family get-togethers.
☐ 9. A major change in financial state (much worse or much better off)
☐ 10. In-law troubles.
☐ 11. A major change in the number of arguments with spouse (regarding child-rearing or personal habits)
☐ 12. Sexual difficulties

The mean values for each life event are on page 13 in the **Stress Evaluation Form**. For items in Part A, check the box for any of the events that happened to you in the past year. Write down only the mean values in the form. For Part B, check the box if it applies to you, also note that Part B events can happen more than once. See the next page to continue.

# PART B

In questions 13-42, indicate the **number of times** (X times) that each event happened to you in the last **two years**, such as 1 or 2 or 3 times.

- ☐ 13. Major personal injury or illness  x_____
- ☐ 14. Death of a close family member (other than spouse)  x_____
- ☐ 15. Death of spouse  x_____
- ☐ 16. Death of a close friend  x_____
- ☐ 17. Gaining a new family member (birth, adoption, older relative)  x_____
- ☐ 18. Major change in the health or behavior of a family member  x_____
- ☐ 19. Change in residence  x_____
- ☐ 20. Detention in jail  x_____
- ☐ 21. Minor violation of the law  x_____
- ☐ 22. Major business readjustment (merger, reorganization, bankruptcy)  x_____
- ☐ 23. Marriage  x_____
- ☐ 24. Divorce  x_____
- ☐ 25. Marital separation  x_____
- ☐ 26. Outstanding personal achievement  x_____
- ☐ 27. Son or daughter leaving home  x_____
- ☐ 28. Retirement from work  x_____
- ☐ 29. Major change in working conditions  x_____
- ☐ 30. Major change in responsibilities at work (promotion, demotion, transfer)  x_____
- ☐ 31. Dismissed from work  x_____
- ☐ 32. Major change in living conditions (moving, new house)  x_____

- ☐ 33. Marital partner beginning or ceasing work outside the home  x_____
- ☐ 34. Taking on a steep mortgage  x_____
- ☐ 35. Taking on a small mortgage  x_____
- ☐ 36. Foreclosure on mortgage or a loan  x_____
- ☐ 37. Vacation  x_____
- ☐ 38. Changing school  x_____
- ☐ 39. Changing line of work  x_____
- ☐ 40. Beginning or ceasing formal schooling  x_____
- ☐ 41. Marital reconciliation  x_____
- ☐ 42. Pregnancy  x_____

*For Part B items, multiply the mean value found on the form on page 13 by the number of times (X times) the event happened, and add up the sum. Then add the totals for Parts A and B in the form on page 13. The more change you have, the more likely you are to be ill.*

WORKPLACE STRESSORS

## Stress Evaluation Form

| Life Event | Mean Value | Your Score | Life Event | Mean Value | Your Score | Life Event | Mean value | Your Score |
|---|---|---|---|---|---|---|---|---|
| 1 | 23 | | 15 | 100 | | 29 | 20 | |
| 2 | 16 | | 16 | 37 | | 30 | 29 | |
| 3 | 15 | | 17 | 39 | | 31 | 47 | |
| 4 | 24 | | 18 | 44 | | 32 | 25 | |
| 5 | 19 | | 19 | 20 | | 33 | 26 | |
| 6 | 18 | | 20 | 63 | | 34 | 31 | |
| 7 | 19 | | 21 | 11 | | 35 | 17 | |
| 8 | 15 | | 22 | 39 | | 36 | 30 | |
| 9 | 38 | | 23 | 50 | | 37 | 13 | |
| 10 | 29 | | 24 | 73 | | 38 | 20 | |
| 11 | 35 | | 25 | 65 | | 39 | 36 | |
| 12 | 39 | | 26 | 28 | | 40 | 26 | |
| 13 | 53 | | 27 | 29 | | 41 | 45 | |
| 14 | 63 | | 28 | 45 | | 42 | 40 | |
| | | | | | | | TOTAL | |

Of those people with a score over 300 for the past year, almost 80% will get sick in the near future; with a score of 150 to 299, about 50% will get sick in the near future; with a score of less than 150, only about 30% will get sick in the near future. Therefore, the higher the score the harder you will have to work to lower your stress.

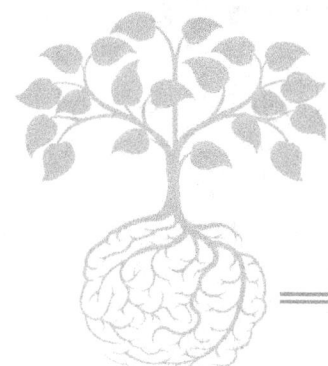

# Chapter 3

## *Illnesses Related To Stress*

David D. Clarke, M.D. discusses baffling illnesses which regularly confront physicians. Dr. Clark labels *Stress Illness* as a 21st century epidemic. In his book, *They Can't Find Anything Wrong*, he states that physicians treat stress illness as a lifestyle rather than connect physical and emotional symptoms as causative.

Symptoms include:

- *Pain from headache, low back/neck, muscle and joint and abdominal pain.*
- *Abnormal swallowing, digestive or bowel dysfunction—from constipation, diarrhea or flatulence.*
- *Nausea and/or vomiting.*
- *Discomfort in the bladder or during urination.*
- *Heart palpitations.*
- *Fatigue.*
- *Sleeping or eating disorders.*
- *Nervous system: blurred vision, dizziness, ringing in the ears (tinnitus), itchy skin, excessive perspiration, and numbness or tingling.*

## Emotions, Stress and Physiology

Aside from the physical symptoms above, emotional stress plays an important role as well. There are five types of stress: from childhood, current lifestyle, post-traumatic, depression, and anxiety.

Identifying the psychological stressors are key to treating the physical components of the illness. If you have one or more of the above physical symptoms, and have a normal evaluation by a physician, then stress can be a cause. Make a list of current stressors in your life with which you have been coping.

### Apply Dr. Clarke's Seven Keys to Treating Stress Illness.

The Seven Keys include:

1. *Know that your symptoms can be diagnosed and treated.*
2. *Consider examining the sources of your stress—make a list of events and places.*
3. *Care for yourself.*
4. *Write your thoughts and emotions down or record them.*
5. *Employ appropriate therapies—medications, counseling or group therapy.*
6. *Overcome hidden resistance to change—list issues.*
7. *Become the person that you were always meant to be.* Overcoming the first six keys will open up your ability to grow and feel confident.

Childhood stress can include issues of abuse to abandonment to negative treatment by peers. Make your own list of specific issues.

Current stressors:
1. *Initially do a Stress Inventory and prioritize important issues.*
2. *Set limits on commitments.*
3. *List possible exercises or things which you enjoy.*
4. *Practice relaxation techniques.*

Symptoms of post-traumatic stress (PTSD) can vary from distressing memories, to nightmares (flashbacks), to anxiety, to feeling detached from the world, to flat affect (depression), to anger.

Depressive symptoms can include fatigue, sleeplessness, difficulty concentrating, and increased irritability.

Anxiety disorders can embrace the above depressive symptoms as well as muscle tension, cold hands and feet, difficulty swallowing, and abdominal discomfort.

There is also a social anxiety disorder which manifests itself as excessive anxiety and self-consciousness in certain social situations. There is fear of embarrassment or judgment by others.

Finally, there is panic disorder which is a limited attack of sudden, intense fear peaking within 10 minutes, followed by at least four of these symptoms—pounding heart, shortness of breath, dizziness, fear of losing control, sweats or chills, numbness or tingling in the hands or feet, nausea or abdominal discomfort.

In summary, pay particular attention to the seven keys, especially #6 regarding hidden resistance:

a. Recognize false beliefs about yourself.
b. Sometimes peers or parents may not respect your efforts to change.
c. If in a relationship, seek support and discuss this with your partner.
d. In a relationship, review your achievements as to whether you deserve better.

Emotions can be transient through thoughts and feelings or constant and intense. Emotions which persist and are not tied to a stimulus are called *moods*. Moods, like depression can persist and negate positive feelings. Emotions have a survival function, namely fear and love without which we could not survive.

## *The Three Parts of the Brain*

Note the diagram of the three parts of the brain and their connections. The three parts are the *cortex*, *limbic* system, and *brain ste4m/autonomic nuclei* which work together for production and maintenance of emotions.

In the *Cortex*, we perceive events and think about them. This information is then sent to the *Limbic System* which stimulates memories through the amygdala and hippocampus to label an emotion to thoughts. The *Brain Stem* regulates the body's response to the emotion produced. The amygdala and hippocampus are most significant in providing a response. The same stimulus to the cortex can evoke opposite emotions depending upon the thoughts and memories stored. Certain emotions such as fear can alert the "flight or fight" response of the Autonomic Nervous System (ANS). The amygdala helps us develop emotional memories in the hippocampus for an appropriate response to a specific stimulus.

## ILLNESSES RELATED TO STRESS

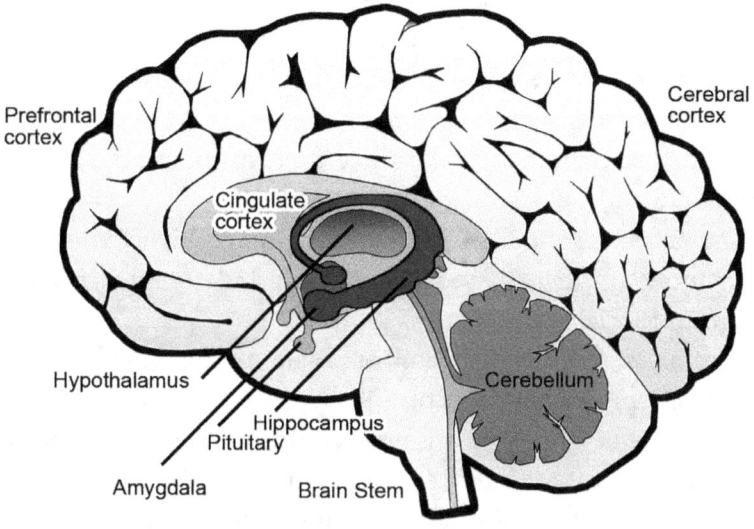

**CORTEX**
⬇ ⬆
**LIMBIC SYSTEM**

Hypothalamus, Amygdala, Hippocampus (Memories of events and emotion to thoughts)

⬇ ⬆
**BRAINSTEM**

Autonomic Nuclei (The reaction to the emotion produced, i.e, how to act, speak, move)

Now for a little basic physiology. The hypothalamus is the ancient part at the base of the brain that reacts to stress by releasing hormones from the pituitary (master gland) and the adrenals (above the kidneys). This increases the heart rate and decreases appetite. The prefrontal cortex (just behind the forehead) is the control center that mediates our cognitive (thinking) abilities—concentration, decision making, planning and ability to retrieve memories. It is sensitive to daily anxiety and worry and is inhibitory to inappropriate impulses.

To further elaborate on the three parts of the central nervous system (CNS):

The *Cortex* or the Conscious Brain governs higher cognition, abstract thought, usage of tools, formation and comprehension of language and social behavior.

The *Limbic System* or Subconscious Brain controls mood, memory and hormone production control. Of the three primary parts of the Limbic system, the *hippocampus* is primarily for memory formation and spatial perception as well. The second part, or *amygdala* is for emotional fight or flight. If the amygdala doesn't function properly, we cannot perceive or exhibit emotions correctly. The third part is the *hypothalamus* for endocrine control, temperature regulation, hunger, thirst, sexual arousal, and the sleep/wake cycle.

The *Brain Stem* or Basal Ganglia, (the Reptilian Brain), provides basic instincts—defending territory and keeping you safe. Major structures are the *substantia nigra, caudate nucleus, putamen* and *globus pallidus*. Pathology of these structures causes ADHD and OCD (obsessive compulsive disorder), Parkinson's disease, Alzheimer's disease and tardive dyskinesia.

According to Laura Pawlak Ph.D., the brain chemicals called neurotransmitters, which exert predominant effect on emotions are *Serotonin, Epinephrine* and *Dopamine*.

*Serotonin* is produced in the raphe nucleus and influences all areas of the cortex, key parts of the limbic system and the brain stem, near the exit to the spinal cord.

*Norepinephrine*, a precursor to epinephrine, is produced in the locus coeruleus (floor of the brain) or pons and hypothalamus which supplies the sympathetic arm of the central nervous system (CNS).

*Dopamine* is produced in the ventral tegmental (motor) area and substantia nigra with branches to the frontal, temporal cortex, basal ganglia and limbic system.

Deficiencies in any three of these neurotransmitters can cause depression. Excess epinephrine stimulated by fear or fright can cause anxiety, panic attacks and specific phobias.

Some neurotransmitters are excitatory, i.e., stimulate brain and body, while others are inhibitory i.e., calm brain and body.

Common stimulants are epinephrine, norepinephrine, dopamine, glutamate, phenethylamine (PEA) and histamine.

Common inhibitors are gamma-aminobutyric acid (GABA), glycine, taurine and serotonin.

Cortisol (from excess stress) stimulates epinephrine but this can be modulated (reduced) by serotonin. Serotonin can be reduced by worry. Dopamine is increased with anxiety and by excess stress or elevated epinephrine. High stress depresses serotonin which in return promotes depression and can cause neuron shrinkage where receptors can decrease and atrophy.

The hippocampus has "stem cells," that when active increase circulation. When information is sent from the prefrontal and temporal cortex to the limbic system, the stimulus is sent through the hippocampus and amygdala where an emotion is assigned to the thoughts. The brain stem then regulates this emotional response. The same stimulus can produce varied responses depending upon the memory. Emotional memories depend on a functioning amygdala in the hippocampus.

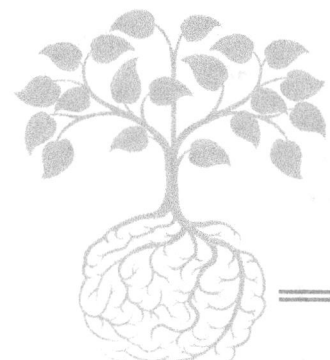

# Chapter 4

## Chronic Stress, Physiology and Solutions

Loretta Bruening, PhD promotes the stimulation of happy chemicals or neurotransmitters:

1. *Defeat the cortisol (survive and thrive)—the bad hormone that guards you from threats so that you can reap rewards. It is better to accept it rather than mask it.*

2. *Oxytocin (Build Trust Consciously). Trust is the trigger—social networks are key to promote good feelings and reward your brain. Trust, verify and repeat. Learn to trust yourself as well as others.*

3. *Endorphin (Do Stretch and Laugh). Pain stimulates endorphin, leading to a short wave of euphoria. It is meant for emergencies. Beyond this, encourage normal secretion through stretching and laughing.*

4. *Dopamine (Embrace a New Goal). Motivates you to meet your needs and promotes persistence. Repeat to create new, positive pathways.*

5. *Serotonin (Believe in Yourself). Confidence in yourself and being respected by others is your reward. Practicing this belief in your self-worth is reinforcement.*

©Florie Freshman

**CONFLICT RESOLUTION NEEDED**

## CHRONIC STRESS, PHYSIOLOGY AND SOLUTIONS

Physiologically, stress is expressed in the body as hormonal, initially through symptoms of hyperexcitability (excess) or ongoing as fatigue (depletion). Hormonal levels can be measured and quantified to include cortisol, DHEA, estradiol (usually), testosterone and progesterone responses.

Remember that stress is cumulative, i.e., the body is affected in the long term and treatment is necessary and in many cases should be a priority especially with accompanying fatigue. The fatigue affects activities of daily living and quality of sleep. Thebody needs time toregenerate hormones and recharge to optimal functioning.

Stress causes the brain to shrink based on a Yale University study. Stress hormones eatawayat the brain tissue—creating miniature holes. In general, cortisol is poised for immediate response to "fight or flight." Chronic stress, however, is not a normal component with which the body can cope on a long-term basis.

The frontal lobe is the most critical for day-to-day functioning. With stress, important aspects will be impaired.

Robert Sapolsky, PhD of Stanford labels the hippocampus as "ground zero" for damage from stress. It governs learning and memory. Fear, anger, love and hate are the primary emotions for storage of memories.

Long-term stress is also associated with certain psychiatric disorders as depression and anxiety. Stress comes from a feeling of having "no control." For some, muscle tension, shallow breathing or headaches can manifest. Dr. Joel A. Holiner, Chief of Psychiatry at Dallas Hospital speaks of difficulty concentrating and inability to make decisions. To move on from high stress, worry or anxiety, take a deep breath and take charge of changes needed.

Use the four-step approach to reduce stress:

1. *When you feel stress coming on, say "Stop" to yourself, and repeat as needed.*
2. *Breathe from the diaphragm deeply, holding your breath and count to ten. Slowly, exhale.*

3. *Focus on the real problem—reflect on the situation.*
4. *Try to find a solution to the problem.*

Break the pattern of escalating worry by evaluation of the problem constructively, planning your approach, and acting to change that which is possible or accepting what you cannot. Connect with others to problem share—achieve a sense of community, and you will be reassured of support. Practice positive self-talk, replacing negative thoughts.

Stress also impacts the body—it can raise cholesterol, constrict your arteries reducing blood flow to the heart, interfere with digestion—from excess acid in the throat to diarrhea, and cause migraines, asthma attacks, and other health problems. Exercise is best for anti-stress, as well as eating healthier and reducing alcohol and caffeine intake. Try to get at least eight hours of sleep—use relaxation techniques to help.

Dr. Holiner advises these anti-stress solutions:

1. *Exercise, which will burn off excess adrenaline to clear the mind.*
2. *Halt ruminating/reliving the same situation.*
3. *Have a support system in operation*
4. *Get sufficient sleep to restore hormonal function.*

Price Pritchett and Ron Pound in "Survival Guide to Stress of Organizational Change," discuss the stress of organizational change with increasingly complex changes. Adapting to these behaviors is the way to combat stress.

*Pritchett and Pound's "Survival Guide" requires you to:*
1. *Put yourself in charge of controlling stress.*
2. *Accept decisions to make changes as needed.*

3. Appear resilient and be productive.
4. Focus on the priorities to be most effective.
5. Seeking low stress organizations may not be in your best interest if the business can fail.
6. Take the position: Accept What We Cannot Change.
7. Review your position to do the right thing for the organization's current goals.
8. Use serious mind control to avoid worry and be productive today.
9. Commit yourself to achieve high standards.

Dr. Herb in relation to stress advises:
1. Recognition of stressor(s) as interfering factors in your life.
2. Specify what ones are most significant.
3. Organize and rectify them through a plan of action.
4. Include a time frame.
5. Retrench or reexamine to determine progress.

According to Drs. A. Marc Gillinov and Steven Nissen of the Cleveland Clinic, stress has a complex relationship with heart disease. The greater the stress, the more likely is the risk of developing heart disease. Stress causes increased blood pressure as well as increased heart rate, and promotes blood clotting. This can lead to a heart attack. It is not conclusive that reducing stress can decrease heart attacks, but is likely to be true.

Emotions can be transient or persistent. Transient emotions are fear, love or pleasure. Emotions which persist can evoke moods, and this can lead to depression and anxiety. Depression can lead to unrelenting sadness, inability to derive pleasure from positive situations and suicidal tendencies.

Anxiety can lead to panic attacks and inability to function in any social setting (agoraphobia).

Acute, uncontrollable stress, however can set off chemical events, can reduce the dominance of the prefrontal cortex, yielding to the older parts of the brain—the hypothalamus. This can cause emotional upheaval from paralyzing anxiety to indulgences in excesses—food, drugs, drink or a spending spree.

Shrinkage in the prefrontal gray matter depends on the length of stress exposure. This chain of events makes us more vulnerable to subsequent anxiety, depression, addiction, and post-traumatic stress (PTSD) whether in battle or at home. In women, estrogen may amplify sensitivity. Women are more likely to be depressed whereas men can succumb to more addictive behaviors and cravings mediated by the basal ganglia.

It seems that our reaction to psychological control under stress is a deciding factor in coping with life. Children growing up in their teens handle stress better if they have successful, multiple experiences as youths and develop resilience. Unfavorable experiences lead to more stress and depression in grownups.

The American Institute of Stress states that 75% to 90% of visits to a primary care physician are stress-related. As stated by the Congressional Prevention Coalition on Stress Prevention, 90% of disease is caused or complicated by stress. Symptoms can range from fatigue, anxiety, anger to weight gain, sleep difficulties, gastric ulcers, and irritable bowel syndrome. More chronic serious problems—heart problems can increase by 40%, heart attack risk by 25%, and stroke by 50%. Additional risks can lead to atherosclerosis, insulin-resistance, immune function disorders, depression and digestive disorders, according to Bill Chioffi, Education Director, Gaia Herbs. Further he states that there are two pathways that affect health—(1) Behavioral and (2) endocrine. Behaviorally, people seem to sleep poorly, smoke more, eat worse, exercise less and do not comply with medical treatment. With endocrine function, immune, nervous and inflammatory pathways predominate.

Fatigue in our society is another common problem. Causes vary—from stress to hypothyroidism, chronic constipation, iron deficiencies, chronic infections, sleep apnea, and trace mineral deficiencies. A simple but temporary solution is aspartate which is used by the brain to transmit nerve impulses and promote energy production in the Krebs cycle. This is combined with potassium and magnesium in a dose of 1 Gm. twice daily as potassium-magnesium taurate, and has restored energy in 75% to 95% of the patients irrespective of the cause. Combining this supplement with behavioral strategies such as meditation, deep breathing and relaxation can reduce the impact of the stress. There is more support from magnesium which can be depleted by stress, high calcium levels, caffeine, some prescription drugs and physical exertion.

Dr. Carolyn Dean calls magnesium the anti-stress supplement. Deficiencies can exacerbate depression, anxiety and feeling cold. Note that serotonin, the "feel good" neurotransmitter depends on magnesium for its production and function.

Nanci Hellmich in USA Today found that older 49 and 50 year old workers plan to reduce job stress. The study was commissioned by Life Reimagined and USA Today through a survey of over 1000 people. About 29% plan to change careers in the next five years—"to give back to society" doing something they've always wanted to do, having flexible hours, and adding schooling. This will restore balance in their lives and provide satisfying experiences to reflect upon.

Stress can cause different responses, depending upon whether it is immediate and temporary or chronic and ongoing. Chronic stress is prevalent in our modern, rapidly changing society where emphasis is on obtaining the most that an individual can contribute to work at the least cost to the business.

Chronic stress is measured through hormonal testing of saliva, blood or urine. Dr. Herb prefers to use saliva since it is reasonably accurate and convenient for the patient to do on their own with simplified instructions. The physician should, however, thoroughly review the instructions with the patient for questions, since incorrect testing invalidates results.

There are three aspects of chronic stress which can manifest depending upon the duration i.e., months to years and the individual response, epigenetic and/or constitutional (inherited makeup) now labeled SNPs (single-nucleotide polymorphisms).

1. *Compensated (Divergent Phase)*
2. *Decompensated (Maladapted Phase)*
3. *Fatigue Phase*

A brief description of each follows:

*Compensated* is the initial phase of chronic stress which manifests in elevated hormonal levels of both total cortisol and free cortisol and a slight increase in cortisol to DHEA ratio. Energy production is mixed—insulin, blood sugar up or down, immune system mostly down—secretory IgA, (NK) Natural Killer cells, other factors—bone loss, protein breakdown, salt/water retention increased.

*Decompensated* is the second phase whereby there is a decrease in free DHEA(S) with similar elevated levels of total and free cortisol and a significant increase in cortisol to DHEA ratio. Insulin sensitivity and glucose utilization are down (as in the initial phase). Similarly blood sugar and gluconeogenesis is up and new hyperlipidemia (unlike initial phase). Immune activity is mostly decreased except for increased antigens and circulating IgG. Other factors are the same as in the first phase.

*Fatigue* is the last phase governed by adrenal exhaustion which can be prevented if caught in time. Total to free cortisol is decreased and free DHEA(S) is normal or reduced. Cortisol to DHEA ratio is decreased as well as gluconeogenesis. Hunger, depression, and low energy are prevalent with symptoms of allergies, inflammation, and degenerative diseases.

Chronic stress can be measured for hormonal components including cortisol, DHEA, fasting and non-fasting blood sugar, sex hormones, and precursors. Subsequently, results are reviewed (salivary and/or urinary testing is more accurate than blood work) and bio-identical hormones prescribed if deficient or certain supplemental products or prescriptions if in excess.

Dr. Herb emphasizes that prolonged (chronic) stress is cumulative and cortisol can then become depleted with serious consequences to bodily functions. This is how lowgrade inflammation can lead to chronic diseases in our society. When stress and fear is chronic, the limbic system, hippocampus and amygdala are continuously activated leading to elevated cortisol. This stimulates the Sympathetic Nervous System which is designed either for (1) real emergencies or (2) perceived threats. The initial immediate response can last for 90 minutes, and takes 30 to 45 minutes to restore to normal, but prolonged stress cannot return the system to normal due to loss of feedback inhibition which is a hallmark of aging. In the latter case, elevated cortisol causes damage as indicated above.

There are various types of stressors in life in which perception of the stress determines the reaction of the individual—from immediate threats to ongoing chronic diseases. There are also social and interactive personal components. Occupational stress is predominant in this society due to instability of worker environments, the economy, and employer concerns about hiring full-time versus part-time workers. Part-time employees, in general, do not receive benefits. There is the push of management to extract 110% from current employees without commitment to ongoing employment, reflecting an unstable economy. This pressure increases on-the-job stress which affects body system functions, including allergies, hypertension, skin disorders, heart, and respiratory diseases.

Emotional stressors are associated with muscle tension and include anger, frustration, with special emphasis on anxiety. Anxiety in particular is correlated with chronic muscle tension. Clinically this can lead to tension headaches, migraines, and musculoskeletal disorders as osteoarthritis (DJD), rheumatoid disease, and possibly Parkinson's disease.

Dr. Herb attended a one-day seminar, "Anxiety Disorders in Children and Adolescents" presented by Christine Dargon, Ph.D. which was thorough and interesting.

Points are:

- *Anxiety is a protective, genetically-preprogrammed emotion that involves survival. It can be helpful to a degree in being resilient, and in alertness and performance.(Sudak, D.M., 2011)*

- *It can be a problem by virtue of biology, personality and stress.*

- *Anxiety disorders and phobias run in families (Muris, 2008).*

- *Anxiety is intimately tied to the physiology of the body.*

- *Neural circuits responsible for conscious self-control are sensitive to even mild stress. When neural circuits shut down, primal impulses predominate and mental paralysis sets in (Amy Arnsten, C. Mazure, and R. Simha).*

- *Patients with anxiety disorders can experience multiple types of anxiety—from panic with or without agoraphobia. They have a higher risk of depression, with a lifetime prevalence of 50-60% having panic disorder as well (Ronald C. Kessler, PhD, et al, 1998).*

- *Co-morbid anxiety and depression can more likely lead to suicide attempts and completion (Myrna M. Weissman, et al, 1988).*

◈ *Substance abuse and dependence follow with potential genetic predisposition for both (Donna M. Sudak, MD, 2011) PTSD can be experienced in children as young as 6 as well as teens. A child can reenact the traumatic experience in play.*

Anxiety disorder can affect 5% to 17% of children and is the most common mental health diagnosis. Overcautious, fearful, and worried symptoms are a problem in the young, whereby parents can play an important role in reducing the fear and anxiety.

There are many techniques available from counselors and/or psychologists to help families or individuals. There are also websites; http://www.pocketmindfulness.com; Jedi Mindfulness Training 3-Step meditation video from Breakthrough Music Therapy Services (https://www.youtube.com/watch?v=NMIw9iE2d5c); and Kids Yoga Online at www.rainbowyogatraining.com.

The human immune system consists of two components:

(1) non-specific or innate immunity toward microorganisms or toxins and (2) specific or acquired immunity toward a particular invader. Principal innate components include white blood cells (granulocytes and monocytes) and natural killer (NK) cell lymphocytes. Primary acquired immunity involves T and B lymphocytes interacting with components of innate immunity i.e., macrophages. There is a psychoneuroimmunological link bridging emotions to brain and immunological responses, i.e., acquired immunity. Therefore psychological stressors can modulate immunity. These stressors can also cause immunosuppression which is temporarily on hold in favor of adrenal cortex response providing glucocorticoids for "fight or flight."

To summarize, emotional stressors can trigger organ system responses which can temporarily adapt. This can, however, progress to prolonged and intense stress causing organ deterioration and leading to chronic infectious and autoimmune disease. The relationship

between our emotions especially in the workplace which occupies 60% to 70%
of our twenty-four hour day can and does influence our relationships both within and outside such environments. It of course can affect family and friends.

Michael Downey, in a June 2012, *Life Extension Magazine* article called "New Reason to Avoid Stress," relates stress to aging, noting that telomeres, which are protective DNA molecules on the ends of chromosomes become shorter. Telomeres are like protective caps on the end of shoelaces which keep the chromosome material from deteriorating or fusing with other chromosomes. When chromosomes divide, telomeres shorten. Eventual shortening is correlated with cellular senescence or aging. Chronic stress can dampen telomerase the enzyme that replenishes telomeres as well as accelerate telomere shortening. Sustained negative stress, e.g, depression can shorten telomeres by 5%.

Chronic negative stress triggers numerous changes throughout the body acting along multiple biochemical pathways including the endocrine, nervous system and immune systems. These can overwhelm the body's balance or homeostasis causing an imbalance. Key biochemical levels can over time be reduced so that symptoms of fatigue, increased susceptibility to illness, job loss and brain fog may manifest.

Specifically the effect of stress on brain function may:

- *Be linked to Alzheimer's where higher cortisol levels are found, causing memory and cognitive impairments.*

- *Cause atrophy of hippocampal dendrites (nerve endings) followed by apoptotic (programmed) death of neurons.*

- *Trigger inflammatory response in the brain which activates pro-inflammatory cytokines IL-4 and IL-6.*

- *Accelerate impairment of cognitive functions.*

- *Cause Post Traumatic Stress Disorder (PTSD), accelerating aging of memory and the body. In magnetic resonance imaging (MRI), the right side of the hippocampal area was found to be 8% smaller in PTSD patients.*
- *Produce chronically high cortisol levels, which are linked to brain damage.*
- *Inhibit the growth of new neurons in the hippocampus.*

Andrew Glanville, D.C. notes that we are born with a capacity to handle stress (stress threshold) throughout our lifetime where our bodies attempt to cope. Two aspects influence reactivity: genetics and the mother's stress in pregnancy and birthing difficulties. The child learns to cope as long as the stress threshold is not exceeded. Later influences, in particular, impatience and anger, physical illnesses, sleeplessness, forgetfulness and/or difficulty concentrating, unusual fatigue and impulsivity signal the need for professional help. Some suggestions to try as well are exercise, escaping the environment, smiling, and discussing it.

# DR. HERBERT I. SCHUCK

©Florie Freshman

**CHILDREN REMEMBER**

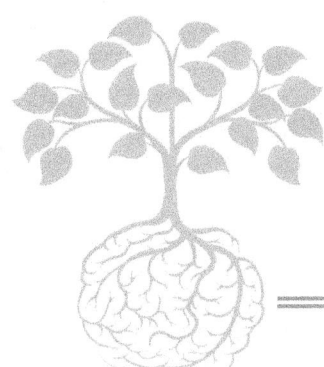

# Chapter 5

## *Parental and Child Relationships*

Parents may think that they hide their stress and worry from their children, but it doesn't work. According to a survey of 1136 young people between 8 to 17 years of age, the children are aware of their parents' behavior—yelling, arguing, or being too busy to spend time with them. Other parents comment that it is better to discuss their challenges with their children, letting them know that they will get through these difficulties together and be OK.

This survey is from the *American Psychological Association*, CEO Norman Anderson.

Top stressors are:

- Money                          76%
- Work                           70%
- The economy                    65%
- Family responsibilities        58%
- Relationships                  55%
- Personal health concerns       52%

- Housing costs                         52%
- Job stability                         49%
- Health problems affecting family      47%
- Personal safety                       30%

Overweight children were more stressed with sleep problems, headaches, anger and fighting. Also these children would eat more when stressed or when going to take a nap. They also exercise less than normal weight children.

We reiterate that anxiety disorders, which can affect 5% to 17% of children, are most common in children. Fear and anxiety can be normal but when children become overly cautious, over-correcting and worried, then it becomes problematic. Girls are more frequently diagnosed than boys.

## Children and Toxic Stress

Current research at Harvard University focuses on studying Toxic Stress of Early Childhood Adversity. There was a seminar presentation on YouTube on three individuals' perspectives:

They were Dr. Jack Shonkoff, the Director of the Center on the Development of Children at Harvard University, Dr. Bob Block, President of The American Academy of Pediatrics, and Roberto Rodriguez, White House Special Assistant to the President on Education Policy.

Dr. Shonkoff defined Toxic Stress as stress response, that when activated becomes chronically stimulated. This disrupts brain circuits and physiologically increases blood sugar, atherosclerosis, insulin resistance, and inflammatory cytokines. The solution is *responsible, protective adults*.

Blocking factors are:

- *Poverty*
- *School failures*
- *Dependence*
- *Lifelong health problems*

Eco-biological developmental research has shown the value of early childhood enrichment programs, but the physiological sources of adversity (above) deny access.

Measuring the payback to society yields favorable statistics to support this research.

Dr. Shonkoff stated that prior focus was on school readiness and primary healthcare. Emphasis needs to be on growing economic inequality, increasing obesity, diabetes and social class disparity. The result is impaired health and development. We need new, protective interventions to enhance the prospects of vulnerable, young children to:

1. *Reduce barriers to learning—child-focused learning and health strategies.*
2. *Build foundations of health.*

Dr. Block Discussed two areas:

1. *The study of education and science of early brain and child development. He emphasized that "[unfortunately] not every child will become an adult (because of diseases and injuries), but every adult once was a child."*
2. *The new science of epigenetics. Epigenetics is the study of environmental effects on genetic predisposition to manifest a particular disease through DNA modifications.*

Dr. Block mentioned that immunizations have removed the threat of many childhood diseases—whooping cough, polio, measles, and others. For example, childhood leukemias were previously a separate entity where only 10% survived, while new treatments provide a 90% survival rate. He said that we also have better intensive care units for trauma cases and disease complications. The Healthcare system, however, with its current high costs is not sustainable.

Children, with exposure to prolonged or severe abuse, neglect, and/or economic hardship are traumatized by the lack of stable, supportive relationships. Healthcare costs need to be redistributed from other programs.

Roberto Rodriguez speaks of early intervention and prevention. There is a need to promote an environment that supports developmental skills through:

- *Home visits for infants and toddlers.*
- *Screening children for toxic stress.*
- *"Headstart" and other programs for children for a better social and emotional foundation.*
- *Coordinating health and educational programs with Health and Human Services.*

K.Herzog in Hamodia, July 16, 2014, discussed a UW (Wisconsin-Madison) study of 128 children divided into four groups: (1) children having experienced physical abuse, (2) children having experienced neglect before being adopted from a foreign country, (3) children from low socioeconomic status, (4) children from typical middle-class without having faced those three types of chronic stress.

MRI scans were done specifically of the hippocampal/amygdala regions of the children's brains. They found a smaller amygdala/hippocampal area among children exposed to some type of the three categories of stress, which definitely relates to early life stresses. As to why this occurs, Jamie Hanson at Duke University Lab for NeuroGenetics will explore a deeper level of brain circuitry upon exposure to these stressors. Hanson hopes to then promote social intervention for these vulnerable children. The brain is changeable and treatable through cognitive therapy, exercise, and medications notes Hanson. In teenagers the brain is still changing and developing until 25 years of age.

A recent study of the relationship of stress and its effect on infertility was published in the March 2014 Journal of Human Reproduction online. Courtney Denning-Johnson Lynch, Director of Reproductive Epidemiology at the Ohio State University Wexner Medical Center found that women with high levels of alpha-amylase were 29% less likely to get pregnant each month and twice as likely to meet the criteria of clinical infertility (not becoming pregnant after 12 months of regular, unprotected sex). They were compared to a group with low levels of alpha-amylase.

Salivary samples were collect on the morning of enrollment and on the first day of their first study-observed menstrual cycle. Both alpha-amylase and cortisol as biomarkers of stress were measured. This was the second study done by Lynch to corroborate the results of more than twice the likelihood of infertility in these women. Lynch promotes yoga, meditation, and mindfulness to reduce stress. Couples need to understand that there are other factors to be considered in addition to stress.

Thea Singer in her book, *Stress Less* initially describes the second phase of the central nervous system response after the "fight or flight" phase whereby the cortex signals the hypothalamus to stimulate the pituitary (master gland) to secrete both CRH (Corticotropin-releasing hormone) and AVP (arginine vasopressin). These then further promote ACTH (adrenocorticotropin hormone) which then activates the adrenal cortex to secrete cortisol (a glucocorticoid) into the circulation. Cortisol then provides glucose from the liver for ongoing energy.

Eventually, high cortisol levels will provide feedback to the hypothalamus to reduce these levels—a negative feedback loop. Beyond this acute situation, chronic stress reduces immune system response—from T helper cells to antibody production. Other functions affected are the cardiovascular and digestive systems.

Any number of conditions on a daily basis can affect these systems—the wear and tear of stress over time, called Allostatic load. The size of this load and our genetic makeup will determine how we progress toward disease.

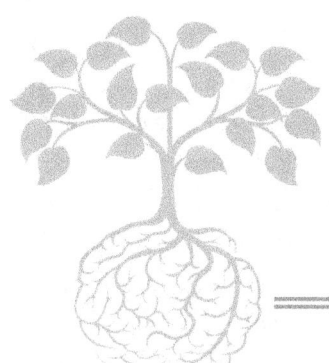

# Chapter 6

## Stress and Telomeres

Elissa S. Epel and Elizabeth H. Blackburn in 2004 wrote a paper on aging and chronic stress such that perception of stress is a marker of how much individuals age, and not external circumstances. Blackburn's studies on telomeres (from Greek *telos* or end and *meros* or part) which are on the ends of chromosomes are a specific marker of aging.

Technically speaking, a telomere consists of four bases—adenine, guanine, thymine, and cytosine (A,T,G,C) which make up the DNA on our chromosomes. These telomeres enable the chromosome to maintain its integrity and become a powerful cancer deterrent. Problems exist when telomeres shorten with each cell division and some of the telomere is lost. This erosion is a sign of aging where their protective function is gone, and no further division is possible. Other biochemical processes eating at the tips are oxidation from reactive oxygen species (ROS), free radicals and inflammation. Environmental factors such as radiation, pollution and UV light can do the same damage.

The body can protect against ROS with internal antioxidants, certain enzymes, vitamin E and vitamin C. Oxidative stress can also damage the telomeres—in particular the mitochondrial DNA.

As telomeres age they either stop dividing (become senescent) or die (exhibit apoptosis). Senescent ones secrete proinflammatory substances and protease enzymes which break down collagen and elastin, thus creating signs of aging. Aging however is complex—telomeres, senescent cells, and hormones work in concert.

Telomerase levels and length in the future may be a better predictor of aging and disease than cholesterol, glucose or CRP (C-reactive protein). Note that telomerase activity is found in 90% of human cancers, so Dr. Judith Campisi, Ph.D., a scientist at California's Buck Institute for Research on Aging, labels it as the "Dr. Jekyll and Mr. Hyde" of enzymes: "compounds like TA-65, which activates telomerase, can certainly in theory have beneficial effects, but they can also in theory have deleterious effects. It's kind of a trade-off. [like many anti-aging techniques.]—they can be both positive and negative depending on time and context, or when and where they're used. There's just no simple answer."

Initially telomere length is influenced by genetics but later environmental and lifestyle factors—smoking, exercise, diet, and infections as well as chronic stress determine longevity. In 2006, Blackburn and Epel found that caregiving mothers with high stress and low telomerase activity had higher blood pressure, cholesterol, fasting glucose, more belly fat, cardiovascular risk factors and elevated hormones. Short telomeres and/or telomerase deficiencies have caused premature aging in specific diseases: Werner Syndrome and dyskeratosis congenital (DC)— short telomeres in idiopathic pulmonary fibrosis.

Drs. Gil Atzmon and Yousin Suh of Albert Einstein College of Medicine studied centenarians who lived exceptionally long lives, finding longer telomere length with the genes coding telomerase having similar mutations to rev up the enzyme's action.

The hippocampus is the seat of memory consolidation and retrieval of declarative or conscious memories and the nearby amygdala—the emotional content of memory, especially fear. For the long-term, memories are stored in the cerebral cortex. Learning can promote the growth of new neurons, but neurons in the hippocampus are especially prone to excess glucocorticoids and Reactive Oxygen Species (ROS) i.e., free radicals which decrease their normal function such that they shut down to protect themselves. In major depression the neurons shrink and the glial cells that nourish the neurons no longer support the neurons. As we age, glucocorticoid levels rise and the hippocampus shrinks, the latter being less likely to shut off the hypothalamus—pituitary— adrenal axis whereby more glucocorticoid is secreted. For example, MRI scans were taken of women forty two to fifty years of age, and then when they were re-scanned in twenty years they had reduced gray matter in the hippocampi (with higher stress scores).

The hippocampus develops early in life—from birth to two years; the amygdala from birth to the twenties, and the cerebral cortex from eight to fourteen years of age. Dr. Sonia Lupien, Ph.D., Director and founder of the Centre for Studies on Human Stress in Montreal, states that the time of exposure to trauma at different times of life will impact on the development of structures through a neurotoxic process, making the brain smaller, and increasing vulnerability to various disease disorders. This then is not necessarily the result of the type of trauma but more so the duration. An example is that women experiencing physical and emotional abuse before twelve years of age have more hippocampal atrophy, whereas women experiencing trauma after twelve years of age have more frontal atrophy. The hippocampal group would suffer memory loss while the cortical group would have impaired reasoning and loss of impulse control.

Chronic stress impairs neurogenesis, the creation of new neurons in the brain. Neurotrophins (growth factors), labeled Brain-Derived Neurotrophic Factor(BDNF) promote growth, proliferation and survival of certain neurons. Glucocorticoids inhibit BDNF under stress.

As the subject is moved from the theoretical to the implementation of coping with stress, Dr. Herb cautions seeking resolution with a practitioner, either a naturopathic or an holistic-oriented physician, who will objectively test the hormonal components. These test kits are available from several laboratories that function under strict

CLIA rules and usually analyze salivary secretions. Urinary testing is available as well. New York has the most stringent regulations and a few of these companies are licensed there. All these laboratories test for stress hormones: cortisol, DHEA, estrogen, progesterone and testosterone. Some of them also have specialty testing—from neurotransmitters to spot testing for cardiovascular disease to female fertility testing. Further information regarding specific laboratories can be found in the Appendix. Once the results of the testing become available to the practitioner, usually in five to seven working days, then treatment can commence.

Treatments can vary: acupuncture is one solution to reduce stress. Dr. Herb prefers to use auricular therapy or Korean hand therapy. Traditional Chinese medicine (TCM) practitioners do traditional meridian therapy. DHEA and/or Hydrocortisone (Rx) may be ordered, depending upon test results. Dr. Herb prefers to use a single herb or some combination of adaptogenic herbs i.e., to adapt to adrenal system overstimulation (compensated) or lowered stimulation (decompensation) by normalizing adrenal function.

Some adaptogenic herbs which can be used are: Ashwaganda, Ginseng, Eleutherococcus, Licorice, Rhodiola, and numerous others. Dr. Herb is versed in the use of kinesiology muscletesting to differentiate the products which test well in order to be more assured of a positive result. He recommends a minimum of three months to one year of treatment, with retesting after three months. This provides the best outcome. There are also two nutrients which reduce stress and enhance attention and productivity: Lemon balm and L-theanine, an amino acid specific to green tea. Lemon Balm has a calming effect in healthy individuals, while L-theanine reduces anxiety. Lemon Balm specifically can enhance cognitive function which may be noted in Alzheimer's patients, 65 to 80 years of age. L-theanine protects brain cells by reducing excitability— enhancing learning, concentration and relaxation.

## STRESS AND TELOMERES

American Fast Food Cravings

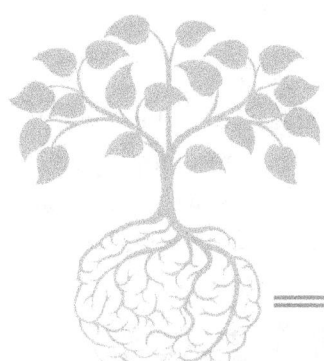

# Chapter 7

## *Food Choices, the GI Tract and Testing*

We can now consider lifestyle changes from the simple—changing your food habits to more involved lifestyle changes which take time and depend on personal motivation.

Food choices are critical for proper metabolic function and energy utilization, especially where fatigue is a predominant symptom. Digestion in the body is both mechanical as well as chemical. The chemical component consists of enzymes which break down large molecules—carbohydrates, proteins and lipids into smaller ones. Digestion begins in the mouth with the salivary glands secreting salivary amylase to break down starches (carbohydrates). In the stomach salivary amylase continues to work as food becomes more liquefied as chyme. Protein digestion begins here with gastric lipase and pepsin which works best at the acidic ph 5 to 6, maintained by HCl of the parietal cells. Secretion of hydrochloric acid (HCl) begins to decline after forty years of age, and affects digestive function.

## Acid Blockers Interfering with Digestion:

Note that H2 blockers such as Ranitidine, Famotidine and others can block the enzymatic activity of HCl in the stomach. Other digestive difficulties as bloating and indigestion can be more appropriately dealt with through the use of digestive enzymes which promote effective breakdown of carbohydrates, proteins and lipids.

## Gluten, Celiac Disease and Testing

There is an increasing number of wheat-sensitive or gluten-intolerant individuals who must avoid these food groups once testing is verified through specific blood work and/or endoscopy. Gluten-intolerant groups are increasing in our society because of more awareness and familial tendencies which become known. There is the influence of genetics or *epigenetics*, i.e., the heritable changes in gene function that do not change the actual genome but act through DNA modifications. According to J. Chasse, N.D. they can occur with various lifestyle behaviors, dietary choices, and environmental exposures. The primary changes occur early on and in childhood: prior to conception, during fetal development, and in puberty. These influence the health of both children and adults.

According to Dr. Alan R. Gaby, M.D., symptoms of gas, bloating, diarrhea, abdominal pain and cramping usually indicate celiac disease also known as gluten-sensitive enteropathy. There is, as well, a non-symptomatic form of celiac disease based on unexplained osteoporosis or an iron-deficient anemia, known as clinically silent type.

Celiac disease is triggered by gliadin—a gluten protein. Ingestion by an individual who is gluten-sensitive causes gastrointestinal damage resulting in malabsorption, destruction of the finger-like villi in the small intestine, and numerous nutritional deficiencies. Other manifestations may include failure to thrive, weight loss, fatigue, anemia, osteopenia or osteoporosis, epilepsy or other neurological disorders, defective gall bladder disease, liver disease (including hepatic steatosis and progressive hepatitis), and infertility. Other celiac-associated diseases may cause autoimmune damage. The most reliable diagnostic test for celiac disease is villous atrophy on small intestinal biopsy. Two different blood tests, Endomysial antibody, IgA (EMA) and Tissue Transglutaminase IgA (TTG) are also used both for diagnostic and screening purposes. Both have a high degree ofsensitivity and specificity. TTG, however, is less costly. Genetic testing can conclusively confirm the antibody tests, since celiac disease is strongly associated with histocompatability leucocyte antigens (HLA) haplotypes types DR3 and DQw2 or HLA-DQ2 and DQ8. To contrast gluten sensitivity from celiac disease, the former may have no gastrointestinal symptoms as well as in "silent celiac disease." In addition, intestinal biopsies may be normal in gluten-sensitive individuals, i.e., no increased intestinal permeability (according to research reported by Dr. Jonathan V. Wright, M.D.). Certain immune markers differentiate the two diseases: immune markers, IL-6 and IL-21 are elevated in celiac disease but not in gluten-sensitivity, whereas TLR 2 is elevated in gluten sensitivity but not in celiac disease. Both do share immune marker FOXP3. This then differentiates the two disease entities, especially in the lack of intestinal mucosal barrier changes. Finally, the antigliadin antibody IgA test is positive in over 90% of these individuals in addition to numerous genetically-related types of diseases—HLA linked. These are almost entirely autoimmune.

Life stresses as infections and imbalances in the gut microflora and micro biome can trigger gluten intolerance. An inflammatory immune molecule, interleukin 17 (IL-17) can cause chronic gut inflammation and dysbiosis (microbial imbalance) in a subset of celiac patients.

Dr. Alessio Fasano, et al (*Lancet* 2000, Apr 29) identified a new immune modulator, *zonulin*, regulator of intestinal permeability which forms tight junctions between cell walls of the gut. Zonulin is present in celiac disease 30 times greater even on a gluten-free diet for two years compared to normals. In other words, this is the "leaky gut" cause. There is also an elevation of zonulin in non-gluten celiac sensitivity (NCGS) comparable to celiacs.

Intestinal bacteria as Salmonella and E. coli stimulate zonulin production and increase the ability of gluten to cause more intestinal damage. This can be harmful to the normal intestinal microbiome where healthy Lactobacillae and Bifidus can restore gluten-induced damage.

Todd Adam Born, N.D. has emphasized the need to test chronically-ill patients for both celiac and type 1 diabetes, as well as testing first degree relatives for celiac disease when they exhibit signs or symptoms. The tests used are total IgA, total IgG, tTG, IgA/IgG, endomysial IgA and DGP IgG/IgG in a panel. If the subjects test to be gluten-free on this panel, he uses genetic testing and subtyping without serology (except total IgA). For non-celiac gluten sensitivity (NCGS), he looks for clinical signs and symptoms. If the subjects are established gluten sensitive, then he suggests a gluten-free diet for three weeks, with a whole wheat challenge three times a day for one day. They are to wait 72 hours (for a delayed reaction). Symptoms arising from the challenge can vary from abdominal pain, headache, or rash to brain fog or irritability. Follow-up of first year patients is more critical than long term patients and symptoms are more common in non-adherent patients. Gluten-sensitive patients should always have their diet reviewed (questionnaires are available). Patients should be given a list of gluten-free foods and gluten-free resources.

Gluten degrading enzymes are provided if cross-contamination takes place.

## FDA's Supervision of Gluten:

The FDA's standard for a food labeled "gluten free" is that it cannot contain more than 20ppm of gluten, but this is only voluntary and not mandatory. People must still scrutinize ingredient lists (*Hamodia* 8-24-2014).

## Low-Fat Diet and Disease Modification:

Dean Ornish, M.D., cardiologist, has extensively utilized a lifestyle intervention program of a strict low-fat diet, regular exercise and stress reduction. He advocates getting 10% of calories from fat with 30 minutes of exercise a day, with yoga to reduce stress or meditation and improving personal relationships. Dr. Ornish challenged Nina Teicholz in her book, *The Big Fat Surprise: Why Butter, Meat, and Cheese Belong in a Healthy Diet*. In her book, she claims that people would welcome the idea that meat and butter—saturated fat— is healthy and plant fats are not. Dr. Ornish contends that there is no research done in this regard. Dr. Robert Atkins, well-known proponent of the ketogenic (low-carb) diet, as well did not provide proof. Dr. Ornish further quotes a 2009 New England Journal Report on mice fed a high-fat, high protein diet vs. a low-fat diet. In the highfat diet, plaque coated the arteries and reduced blood flow almost completely.

Dr. Ornish co-published with Elizabeth Blackburn in *Lancet Oncology* a study of men who followed the Ornish program, who significantly increased the length of their telomeres— (short telomeres being a sign of aging). In earlier research his program had shown reversal of heart disease, type 2 diabetes and early-stage prostate cancer.

# DR. HERBERT I. SCHUCK

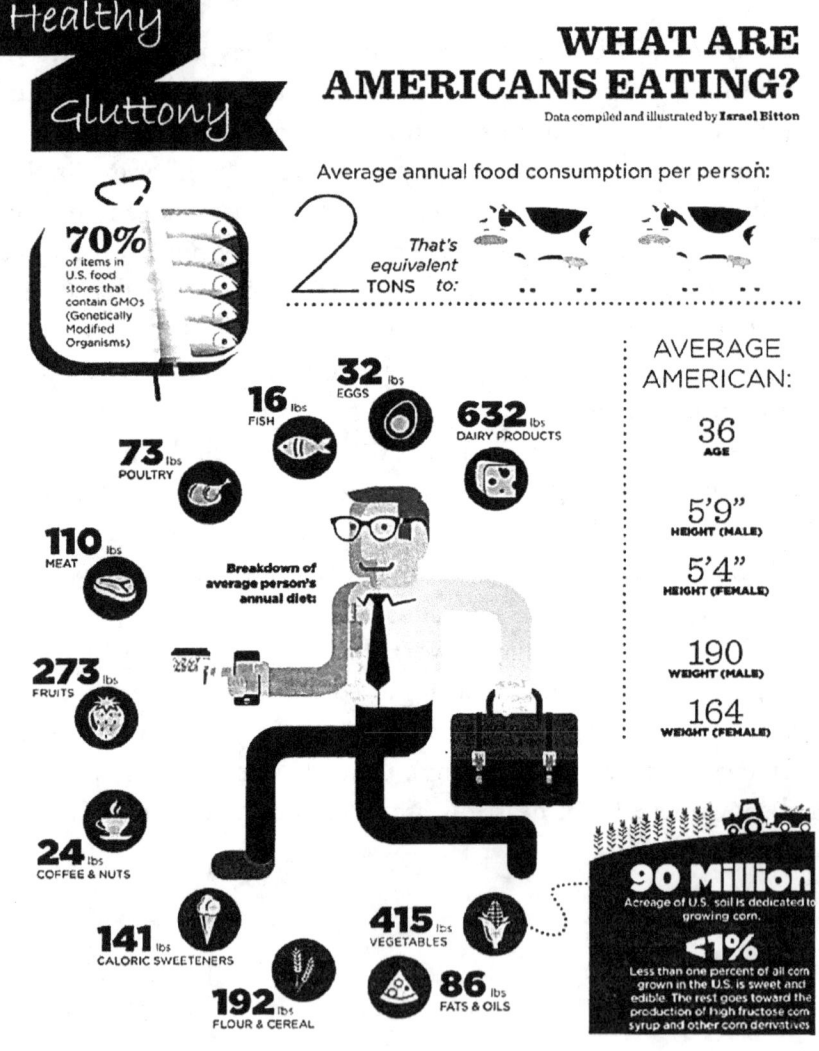

## Irritable Bowel Disease (IBD), IBS and SIBO

Gary Weiner, N.D., L.Ac., in NDNR, January 2016, has defined differences between IBD, IBS, and SIBO.

IBS is usually functional or lacking overt symptoms whereas IBD generally has specific symptoms as does SIBO. Dr. Weiner has found symptoms in IBS as well, due to inflammation which drives immune function but with less intensity. IBD patients can have abdominal bloating, stomach pain, diarrhea, and excessive gas production. IBD in remission can have IBS-like symptoms of constipation or bloating.

## SIBO:

There is a G.I disease entity which can mimic IBS, and that is SIBO, small intestinal bacterial overgrowth. The small intestine is the longest section of the gastrointestinal tract through which nutrients are absorbed. With SIBO causing malabsorption, assimilating adequate levels of fat-soluble vitamins and iron can be a problem. Bacteria can then invade the small intestine, leading to IBS-type symptoms and damage to the stomach lining. Treatment with antibiotics does not cure, since it kills the good bacteria as well. Probiotics and probiotic-rich food assist with digestion and absorption of nutrients (pilot study at Center for Medical Education and Clinical Research, Buenos Aires, Argentina) and 82% of those on probiotics reported clinical improvement, while only 52% percent receiving antibiotics reported clinical improvement. A low FODMAPS diet is suggested for two weeks (see following). Additional suggestions are: stress reduction, acupuncture, eating fermented foods such as sauerkraut with meals. Organic coconut oil is healthy.

When antibiotic treatment with rifaximin fails, oregano, berberine and lemon balm oil are effective as herbs.

IBS and IBD both have microbiome disturbance. SIBO can affect IBS. Drs. Pimental, Sandberg-Lewis and Siebecker note that relieving the symptoms of SIBO by treating the microbiome through antimicrobial, dietary and prokinetic support clears the IBS symptoms. Dr. Weiner elaborates specific lab tests, and provides cases.

## Biomarkers for IBD:

Timothy K. Lu, Oliver Purcell, Christopher Voight and others at M.I.T have been working with mice and a bacterium, *Bacteroides thetaiotaomicron*, frequently found in high levels in the gut of 50% of adult humans. The microbe uses part of its DNA to scope out the gut for a predetermined substance. The product was fed to the mice beforehand, and the mice excrete the product in their droppings. The microbes glow under a microscope if they have encountered their target. The substance reported could be something toxic or a bio-marker. IBD or early cancer could thus be reported.

Recently IgG food allergy testing has also proven of value by enabling the elimination of foods with a positive reactivity. The test is called *enzyme-linked immunoabsorbent assay* (ELISA) and requires a blood draw. Symptom improvement can be up to 75% for asthma, coughing, tinnitus, chronic fatigue, headaches, gas, bloating, diarrhea, skin rash, itching and nasal congestion. More importantly, irritable bowel syndrome (IBS) and Crohn's disease has also benefited from the IgG elimination diet.

Because IgG food allergy to wheat, gluten, gliadin, rye and barley exist in celiac disease, people with celiac disease routinely exhibit elevated IgG antibodies after consuming wheat or grains. Celiac disease, according to Marios Hadjivassiliou, M.D. et al, can be a subtype of wheat sensitivity. Many of his patients who are positive for wheat allergy but negative for celiac disease had neurological symptoms which resolved with gluten elimination. For patients who test IgG positive for gluten, their symptoms can affect autism, bipolar symptoms, depression, schizophrenia, migraine headaches, asthma, and obesity.

Bethany Glynn, N.D. in Townsend Letter of Jan. 2014, discusses celiac disease and gluten-associated conditions. She notes the controversy as to whether IgG antibodies can be used to assess patients for food allergies. Testing IgA as a non-IgE mediated marker of food allergy is preferred.

Salivary IgA exists in the gut and releases lymphocytes to protect against pathogens. It can be used as a measure of an immune-mediated reaction to gluten, especially where patients have atopic dermatitis and urticaria. Total IgA can be elevated during inflammation, inflammatory bowel disease (IBD), connective tissue disease or metabolic syndrome. Anti-TTG IgA is a marker for diagnosis of celiac disease. IgG is more a marker of immune tolerance than allergy EAACI (Europe). IgE is a classic measure of immune response with histamine release and the potential for anaphylaxis.

## FODMAPS:

A gluten-like reaction from wheat, rye, and other grains called FODMAPS can cause excessive gas and pain. In an Australian study, in cases of probable gluten-sensitivity, it was found that it may be FODMAPS that are responsible for the bloating and flatulence. However, since FODMAPS occur with gluten in many foods, we don't know precisely what is triggering the reaction.

FODMAPS is an abbreviation for *Fermentable, Oligo-, Di-, Mono-saccharides and Polyols*, which are short-chain carbohydrates that are poorly-absorbed by some people in the small intestine. These carbohydrates can cause abdominal pain, bloating, constipation and/or diarrhea, gas and digestive sensitivities.

The Monash University and Nestle Health Science websites list certain high FODMAPS foods and their low FODMAPS substitutes:

- *http://www.med.monash.edu/cecs/gastro/fodmap/lowhigh.html*
- *https://www.nestlehealthscience.us/lowfodmap/fodmap-101.*

## Some high-FODMAPS foods include:

Asparagus, artichokes, onions, leek, garlic, peas/beans, onion and garlic salts, beetroot, Savoy cabbage, celery, sweet corn, apples, mango, pears, watermelon, nectarines, peaches, plums, cow's milk, yoghurt, soft cheese, cream, custard, ice cream, rye, wheat, cashews, pistachios, High fructose corn syrup, honey and agave.

## Some low-FODMAPS foods include:

Alfalfa, bean sprouts, green beans, bok choy, bell pepper, carrot, chives, fresh herbs, cucumber, lettuce, tomato, zucchini, banana, orange, mandarin, grapes, melon, lactose-free milk, lactose-free yoghurts, hard cheese, meats, fish, chicken, tofu, tempeh, gluten-free bread, sourdough spelt bread, rice, oats, gluten-free pasta, quinoa, almonds and pumpkin seeds Research at Monash University, Victoria, Australia, on 37 subjects with non-gluten sensitivity (NCGS) and on low FODMAPS diet and crossover study reduced G.I. symptoms. A 16 month study at University of Otago, NZ of patients diagnosed with IBS also showed decreased bloating, flatulence and diarrhea.

# FOOD CHOICES, THE GI TRACT AND TESTING

## How much food gets wasted?

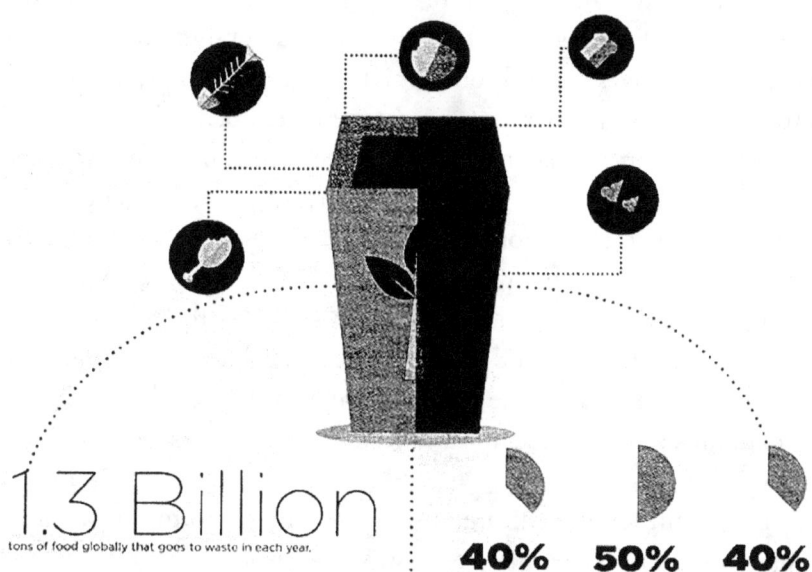

**1.3 Billion**
tons of food globally that goes to waste in each year.

That's **4x** the amount needed to feed the nearly 1 billion people in hunger globally.

**40%**
Of food grown or raised in the U.S. is not eaten.

**50%**
The percentage rise of food waste in the U.S. since 1974.

**40%**
Of landfill contents in the U.S. comes from food waste

**$165 Billion**
worth of food in the U.S. that goes to waste

**1/3**
Of the global food supply is wasted.

**17%**
The amount of food diners throw to waste from their meals in restaurants.

**25%**
Amount of food per household that goes to waste in the U.S.

**$2,275**
Average cost of wasted food per household.

DR. HERBERT I. SCHUCK

## Food Allergies and Food Intolerance

## Food Sensitivities:

Natural chemicals found in nature were discussed by Drs. Anne Ruth Swain, V.I. Soutter and R.H. Loblay, in the Allergy Unit of the Royal Prince Albert Hospital entitled, "The Complete Guide to Avoiding Allergies, Additives, and Problem Chemicals," Sydney, Australia. Certain individuals can still react to these chemicals, but it is less likely when eating a balanced diet. Infections, binges on specific foods, or sudden changes in diet can increase reactivity. There is a familial tendency to promote food sensitivity as well. Women tend to be more reactive, possibly related to hormone changes during child-bearing years. Even natural chemicals in "healthy foods" can react with people similarly to food additives in artificial foods. Note should be made that the tastier the food, the higher the possibility that it will contain sensitizing chemicals and thus have greater potential for reactivity.

Dr. Swain, et al, indicates specific chemicals common to food groups to which people may be sensitive and react.

## Chemicals causing sensitivities:

Salicylates *are found in fruits, vegetables, nuts, herbs, and spices, jams, honey, yeast extracts, tea and coffee, juices, beer, and wine. Salicylates are also in flavorings (e.g., peppermint), perfumes, scented toiletries, eucalyptus oils, and some prescriptions, (e.g., aspirin–acetylsalicylic acid).*

Amines *arise from protein breakdown or fermentation. There are large amounts in cheese, chocolate, wines, beer, yeast extracts and fish products. They are also present in certain fruits and vegetables, such as bananas, tomatoes, avocados, and broad beans. Amines are also made internally, (e.g., adrenaline).*

Monosodium glutamate (MSG) *is a building block of all proteins. It is found naturally in most foods. In its free form, not linked to protein, it enhances the flavor of foods.* Foods rich in MSG are tomatoes, cheese, mushrooms, stock cubes, sauces, meat and yeast extracts. It may be found as an additive in soups, sauces, Asian cooking, and snack foods. One caveat: it can affect neurologic (brain) function causing hyperactivity in susceptible individuals especially children. It has been known to cause, "Chinese restaurant syndrome" which can manifest in headaches, agitation, asthma, chest tightness, increased heart rate, tingling in muscles and skin, and mood swings.

People who react to natural food chemicals are also likely sensitive to food additives: in addition to monosodium glutamate (MSG), there are sorbates, benzoates, sulfites, nitrites, and propionates (most commonly used as preservatives for food freshness). These can cause allergic or asthmatic reactions and hyperactivity in susceptible individuals, especially children. Colorings are also included, and can be natural or artificial. A natural coloring agent used is *annatto* which *usually* has no toxicity. Similar reactions to preservatives can occur as well.

Reactions to food chemicals are not allergies but food *intolerance*. They irritate nerve endings in different parts of the body, like drug specific side effects. Symptoms vary from hives, to mouth ulcers, stomach pains, or abdominal pain, and headaches. Others effects may be flu-like symptoms and/or tiredness. Children can exhibit irritability and restlessness. Exposure to rich foods, heavily-colored foods, flavored or preserved food and drinks can also promote these symptoms. Highly-sensitive individuals should avoid these products.

Allergies are generally defined as immediate or delayed reactions which can manifest with similar symptoms, especially urticaria (hives) and airway tightness which may require emergency treatment and intubation. It can thus be difficult to differentiate food intolerance from food allergies based on symptoms alone. Allergy testing may confirm specific substances or reactants. Food allergies are reactions by antibodies to food proteins. In familial cases, the triad of eczema, hay fever, and asthma are common. Common reactants are wheat, eggs or milk. Peanuts are also a common allergen. Note that there are environmental stressors—pollens including trees and grasses, chemical pollutants, molds, animal hairs, and dust which the body interprets as a "foreign invader." There is then an antigenantibody reaction,(Ag-Ab) i.e., antibodies to defend against the antigen whereby either histamine or chemicals are released to fight inflammation. Organs affected are mainly the skin, mucous membranes, lungs, and gastrointestinal tract. Symptoms commonly experienced are itchy, watery eyes, runny and congested nose/sinuses, skin reactions (urticaria), and rapid heart rate. Less frequent symptoms are headache, fatigue, intestinal gas or pain, abdominal bloating, and mood swings (see Hass, Elson,M.D. and Levin, Buck, Phd, *Staying Healthy With Nutrition*, 2006).

Food intolerance does not involve the immune system as does allergies, according to D. Orlick Levy who lists common foods leading to intolerance: beans, cabbage, citrus-fruit, glutencontaining foods, lactose from milk or dairy products, and processed meats. About 7% of children and 7% of adults have a food allergy. Most children outgrow their food allergies when they become adults. It is noteworthy that peanut and treenut allergies as well as fish and shellfish allergies are lifelong, whereas cow's milk and soy allergies can subside by 16 years of age. About 10% of adults are lactose intolerant.

Yale Tusk, M.Sc. reviewed current research on "Breakfast as the Most Important Meal of the Day," July 2016. It seems that there is no scientific evidence to support this proposal that has been with us from Roman times. The Romans only ate one meal a day (approximately at noon)—any more than that was considered gluttony at that time. Their society was obsessed with digestion. The Greeks ate just two meals daily, and they were strong and mentally proficient, as did the ancient Hebrews.

However, in a study in 2014, in the *American Journal of Clinical Nutrition*, of 309 adults who were obese were broken into two groups, half skipped breakfast and the other ate breakfast over four months. No difference was found in weight loss. In fact, the U.S. Dietary Guidelines in 2010 regarding breakfast stated that *children who don't eat breakfast are at greater risk of obesity. Evidence is stronger in teens.* Linda Van Horn, Professor at Northwestern University and chair of the *2010 Advisory Committee,* stressed the value of breakfast in terms of high-fiber intake which is lacking in American diets.

We do still not have well-designed studies on whether breakfast actually influences health.

There is some rationale, however, for "intermittent fasting," without reducing overall calorie consumption. This is done whereby the body can only burn stored fat once digestion is complete. The longer the interval between dinner and breakfast—minimally 12 hours—the more weight will be lost. Even more weight is lost by increasing the span to 13 to 14 hours. If hunger occurs, fresh vegetables or fruits can be a solution.

Dr. David Lustig, M.D., PhD, Harvard Medical School, states that "intermittent fasting" can improve insulin sensitivity and produce ketones, a kind of super fuel for the body and brain. Ketones are normal, though, when fasting or eating low-carbohydrate foods. Dr. Lustig emphasizes that there are no long-term studies. He advocates reducing carbohydrates, especially processed grains, starchy potato products and added sugars. For those individuals with no appetite in the morning for breakfast, a cup of tea with lemon, water or coffee without sugar can give a lift until lunch. To elaborate on the subject of breakfast, it should be noted that Dr. Greg Phillips, Dean of Science, Engineering and Math at Blinn College, Texas, explored the breakfast eating habits of 1,259 college students. Over eleven years, the study found that "there was a significant difference in the performance on the exam with a higher percent of the participants who had eaten breakfast passing the exam." (see "Does Eating Breakfast Affect the Performance of College Students?").

Dr. Alan R. Gaby, M.D. has noted a new disease entity, Eosinophilic Esophagitis (EE), in the January 2013 *Townsend Letter.* It is a chronic inflammatory disease characterized by eosinophilic

## DR. HERBERT I. SCHUCK

infiltration of esophageal epithelium. Esophageal strictures are commonly found on endoscopy. EE occurs both in children as well as adults. In Western society it has the same incidence, 40 to 55 per 100,000 as Crohn's disease.

# How to Get GMOs Off Your Plate

**9 INGREDIENTS TO WATCH**

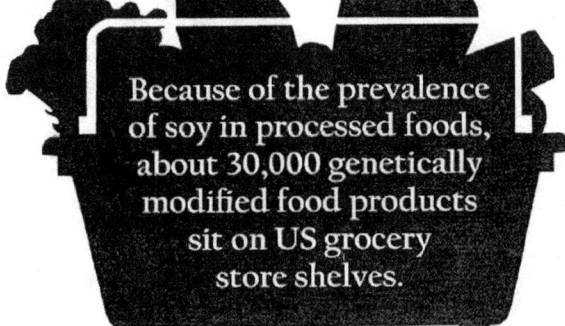

Because of the prevalence of soy in processed foods, about 30,000 genetically modified food products sit on US grocery store shelves.

**① SOY**
**GM since:** 1996
**How widespread:** 94 percent of the US soybean crop was genetically modified in 2011, according to the USDA.
**What to watch for:** Soybeans, genetically modified for a lower trans-fat content, show up in many traditional (i.e. not organic) soy products, such as tofu, soy milk, soy sauce, miso, and tempeh, as well as any product containing the emulsifier lecithin (often derived from soybean oil), such as ice cream and candy.

**② COTTONSEED**
**GM since:** 1996
**How widespread:** 90 percent of the US cotton crop was genetically modified in 2011, according to the USDA.
**What to watch for:** The cotton plant, genetically modified to be pest-resistant, produces not only fibers for fabric, but also cottonseed oil, available on US shelves as a standalone product, and also commonly used as an ingredient in margarine, in salad dressings, and as a frying oil for potato chips and other snacks.

**③ CORN**
**GM since:** 1996
**How widespread:** 88 percent of the US corn crop was genetically modified in 2011, according to the USDA.
**What to watch for:** Corn has been modified for a number of different reasons: to resist herbicides, pesticides, and insects, and also for enrichment of vitamin C, vitamin B9, and beta carotene. GM corn can make its way into hundreds of products: breakfast cereals, corn-flour products (tortillas, chips, etc.), corn oil products (mayonnaise, shortening, etc.), and literally anything sweetened with high-fructose corn syrup, which covers sweetened fruit drinks, processed cookies and other snacks, yogurts, soups, condiments, and many other products.

**④ CANOLA OIL**
**GM since:** 1996
**How widespread:** 90 percent of the US canola crop was genetically modified in 2010, according to the New York Times
**What to watch for:** Any canola oil made in the USA. This popular cooking oil, originally derived from rapeseed oil by breeders in Canada (the name is a contraction for "Canadian oil, low acid") comes from a genetically modified plant that is no longer simply cultivated, but grows wild across the Dakotas, Minnesota, and Canada.

**⑤ U.S. PAPAYA**
**GM since:** 1998
**How widespread:** 80 percent of the US papaya crop was genetically modified in 2010,

according to the New York Times.
**What to watch for:**
All papaya grown in the US. Hawaiian papaya was genetically engineered to withstand the ringspot virus in the late 1990s, with the GM version rapidly taking over the industry. In 2009, the USDA rescinded regulations prohibiting GM papaya on the US mainland; they have since been introduced to Florida plantations.

**⑥ ALFALFA**
**GM since:** In 2005, the USDA deregulated GM alfalfa, though cultivation was later halted in 2007, following lawsuits from the Center for Food Safety and others who demanded a full evaluation of the threats to conventional alfalfa plants, and the emergence of herbicide-resistant weeds

Clinically, signs and symptoms vary with age. In infants, food refusal (usually due to dysphagia) is common. Children manifest with heartburn, vomiting, reflux, and abdominal pain. Teenagers and adults have dysphagia and food impaction. Clinically symptoms resemble acid reflux (GERD), however EE does not respond to acid suppression. Food allergy in EE patients is common to most of them. A six-food elimination diet (SFED) is advocated to identify symptom-evoking foods. The six foods listed are milk protein, egg, soy, wheat, peanuts/tree nuts, and fish/shellfish. 50 patients on SFED also avoided foods identified through clinical history and skin pricks tests. Dysphagia improved in 94% of which 64% were labeled as histologic responders.

The most common food triggers were wheat (60%), milk (50%), soy (10%), nuts (10%), and egg (5%). In other studies corn and beef were common allergens. Adults with EE usually react to one food, whereby children react to more than one. 15% of the children reacted to almost all foods tested. In those patients a hypoallergenic, amino acidbased, elemental diet is promoted to ensure remission.

A combination of skin prick tests and atopy patch was as reliable as an elimination diet in diagnosing food allergies in EE children. This method is unreliable for adults and children over 14 years of age where an elimination diet is essential.

## Overuse of antibiotics:

The overuse of antibiotics is commonly linked to Candida albicans (yeast) infections. This, in turn, can also stimulate the formation of antibodies to gluten as well as autoimmune antibodies against tissue transglutaminase (TTG) and endomysial antibodies in gluten-sensitive individuals. This was reported by Dutch researchers in 2003. In 2009, researchers treated *Candida albicans* in a four-year old boy with anti-fungal medications which reduced the antigliadin antibodies as well. A recent study at the University of Manitoba, Canada found that babies in the first year of life who receive antibiotics are three times more likely to experience IBD (irritable bowel disease) later in life. Furthermore, these researchers hypothesized that it is the disturbance of bowel flora which can lead to IBD. Dr. Charles Bernstein, Director of the IBD Research Centre cautioned the use of antibiotics for infants, especially with a family history of IBD.

**Lack of food and critical development:**

R.W. Miller in USA Today has highlighted an ongoing problem with teenagers—hunger to the point of starvation and deprivation of critical nutrients due to extreme poverty. Teens resort to selling drugs or sex as well as stealing to survive. Neville Golden, chief of adolescent medicine at Stanford and on the American Academy of Pediatrics nutrition committee notes that teenage years are the time that development and growth predominate outside of the first year of life.

## *Allergies and GMOs*

A new report by Jeffrey Smith and Tom Malterre, M.S., C.N. of the Institute for Responsible Technology (IRT) on the connection between Genetically Modified Organisms (GMOs) in foods and gluten sensitivity states that as many as 18 million Americans can be affected by gluten.

The authors state that GMO foods may trigger or exacerbate gluten-related disorders as well as celiac disease in five conditions:

1. *Intestinal permeability.*
2. *Imbalanced gut bacteria.*
3. *Immune activation and allergic response.*
4. *Impaired digestion.*
5. *Damage to the intestinal wall.*

## A note on hybridized wheat:

Though wheat is hybridized, it is not a GMO food, the latter requiring insertion of a gene—from animal, or vegetable source into its DNA. Hybridized wheat, however, has been found to be more allergenic to individuals when compared to the original wheat, e.g, kamut because of the way it is doused with glyphosate at many stages of harvest—including preharvest (see *Monsanto's Preharvest Staging Guide use of Roundup*).

GMO foods currently modified are soy, cotton (cottonseed oil), corn, canola oil, sugar from sugar beets, zucchini, yellow squash, Hawaiian papaya, and alfalfa. The fact that Monsanto resists labeling of GMO foods is an insult to the freedom of full disclosure. It seems to imply a hidden agenda. Furthermore, GMOs are engineered to tolerate a weed killer, glyphosate (Roundup) which still remain at high levels in the crop at harvest (see "What Do We Really Know About Roundup Weed Killer?" by Elizabeth Grossman, *National Geographic*, April 23, 2015).

GMO Corn and cotton have an insecticide called Bt-toxin. Bt-toxin is supposed to punch holes in insect cells. The irony is that it does the same in humans, thereby leading to "leaky gut" which appears in gluten-sensitive individuals. Emily Linder, M.D. states that she finds treatment of gluten-sensitive patients is faster and more complete when GMO foods are removed from their diet.

Dr. Jonathan Wright, M.D. in July 2012 *Nutrition & Healing*, has written extensively on GMOs. He indicated that the latest incursion of patenting specific foods by major companies as Monsanto and Dow Chemical whose major purpose is control and profit from our food supply. GMO is not a natural way to grow—the insertion of the "genome" or DNA from one species into the genome of another which create a new set of genes unlike the original. This was first done in 1973 with recombinant E. coli bacteria.

The current controversy is creation of current "patent protected" food crops by five primary companies: Monsanto, DuPont, Syngenta,

Bayer Crop Science and Dow, the "'Ag Biotech" group. These "patented plants" contain "stacked traits" for dual purposes:

1. *Be herbicide resistant so weed-killers used around them are protected.*

2. *Produce internal proteins not naturally present so they are less susceptible to pests but supposedly harmless to humans.*

Unfortunately, "patent-protected" plants have genetic combinations not normally present in Nature: their native protective mechanisms are over-ridden. The "group" claims morenutrition and higher yields. The risks of creating unknown food entities have not been fully disclosed. Safety testing has been limited to 90 days only in lab animals. The tests are not mandatory nor are they independently verified.

Reviewers of GMO research have raised questions about health risks for GMO soy, rapeseed oil (Canola), and corn genetically altered to resist Monsanto's Glyphosate ("Roundup"). The research data is inadequate to project safety for those with chronic health problems. This same reviewers have noted potential danger for liver and kidney toxicity. They disparage the limited 90-day studies not being extended and independently evaluated.

In 1999, independent researchers in Britain at the government's request assessed GMO engineered potatoes to make a "lectin" called GNA (Galanthus nivalis agglutinin) lectin. After 10 days consumption in rats, there was enlargement of their pancreas and intestines and beginning atrophy of their livers. Animals fed non-GMO potatoes were unaffected. There were attempts to bury the results and the lead researcher was fired.

In 2003 an independent review group reported that after review of the data, damage to the rats' internal organs was not due to the potatoes or the GNA lectin but "the genetic modification process itself." In a 3-month feeding trial of Monsanto GMO corn, MON 863, on rats, they showed significant changes in blood sugar, absolute lymphocyte and white blood cells and absolute basophils but it was not biologically relevant at the end. These values would raise a danger signal to a physician since they could cause allergies, infection and diabetes. An independent research group by German court order for MON 863 (see Archives of Environmental Contamination and Toxicology, May 2007, Volume 52, Issue 4, pp 596–602) found hidden data showing hepatorenal toxicity, increased triglycerides and decreased urinary phosphorus and sodium. The conclusion of the research was that a 90-day study was inadequate for safety determination. A longer study was needed: "with the present data it cannot be concluded that GM corn MON863 is a safe product." (see "New Analysis of a Rat Feeding Study with a Genetically Modified Maize Reveals Signs of Hepatorenal Toxicity," Séralini, GE, et al, May, 2007).

Recent studies in 2012 of "stacked traits" i.e. more than one intentional DNA modification, with corn used a subset of B-t toxins—"Cry 1 Ab" and "Cry 1 Ac". Side effects with human embryonic stem cells were observed with "Cry 1 Ab" at 100ppm leading to cell death; Cry 1 Ac had no effects. Glyphosate was also studied for toxicity in human embryonic stem cells with dilutions as low as 50 ppm. This caused cell death—at this dilution which is far lower than normally used for agriculture. There are other studies that a key ingredient in "Roundup" causes endocrine (hormone) disruption, and could pose a risk for cancer. Monsanto and the "Ag Biotech" group denies it.

There are "promoter" genes to "turn off" or "turn on" existing genes in all natural plants, the results of which are unpredictable. The promoter used in most GMO crops is the cauliflower mosaic virus (CaMV). There is evidence to this fact. Furthermore, a study suggests that GMO genes can travel or transfer into intestinal or human cells. Researchers found soy genes in the gut bacteria of three out of seven study volunteers who had ileostomies (removal of the lower small intestine with feces collected in a bag). Results were inconclusive, since transgenes were not found in the fecal matter. The transfer could have occurred before the study.

However, transgenes have been found in rat studies as much as 3 days later after initial feeding. (see "DNA stability in plant tissues: implications for the possible transfer of genes from genetically modified food." Chiter A, et al, Sept 15, 2000)

High risk GMO crops are as follows:

- *Alfalfa—all since 2011*
- *Canola—90% of US production*
- *Corn—88%*
- *Cotton—90%*
- *Papaya—most of Hawaiian crops*
- *Soy—94%*
- *Sugar beets—94%*
- *Zucchini and Yellow Summer Squash—25,000 acres*
- *Milk, meat, eggs and honey conventionally-raised are a high risk for GMO ingestion where animals are fed from these crops.*

Moderate risk foods and crops either from cross-pollination or contamination include chard, beets, rutabaga, Siberian kale, bok choy, mizuna, Chinese cabbage, turnip, acorn squash, flax and rice.

GMO derivatives can be aspartame, ascorbic acid, high fructose corn syrup (HFCS), amino acids, hydrolyzed/textured vegetable protein, sucrose, and yeast products.

Note was made of headlines in the London Daily Mail: "Thousands of farmers from India committed suicide due to failure of GMO crops in 2011." The farmers were promised high yields and more income to switch from traditional seeds to GM seeds. There were overwhelming failures and no income. The result: 125,000 farmers committed suicide. The initial pressure to use India as a testing ground for GMO's failed.

In the January/February 2014 issue of *Green America* there is an article entitled "Farmers vs. Corporate Seed Police," where Monsanto sends out "seed police" to inspect farms on farmers who did not purchase GM seeds or plants from the company. If farmers saved the seeds from the harvest (farmers usually recoup seeds from a normal crop for the following year), Monsanto sued them for patent infringement and took them to court even if they claimed it was accidental.

The Center for Food Safety in 2013 report found that Monsanto also went after seed cleaners who helped farmers save non-patented seeds. Between 1997 and 2010 Monsanto filed 144 lawsuits and settled 700 more cases out of court, according to OSGATA (Organic Seed Growers and Trade Association). Farmers are concerned about cross-pollination from insects, wind and farmer error which can contaminate non-GMO and organic crops. They need to meet minimum standards to sell overseas or to non-GMO project certified sources.

## Biotech Monopoly:

53% of the global commercial seed supply is owned by three biotech companies: Monsanto, Syngenta and DuPont. This has led to higher seed prices for farmers—by 325% to plant one acre of soybeans, 516% for cotton, and 259% for corn in a 2013 report from the Center for Food Safety, "Seed Giants vs. US Farmers." This is worrisome for farmers. There is also a decrease in seed diversity, especially when it comes to GMOs. There is less variety of crops where genetic diversity forges resistance to weather and diseases.

We are replacing natural diversity with patented GMOs of a few genetic lines. A pittance of GM strains make up 90% of US corn, 93% of soy, and 90% of cotton.

We are on a pesticide treadmill—GMOs are responsible for increased pesticide use. Water pollution, soil contamination, and risks to farmworker health are further problems. In January 2014, a bulletin from Dow revealed that "86% of the corn, soybean, and cotton growers in the South have herbicide-resistant or overabundance of weeds on their farms." More studies indicate GM pesticides can be harming pollinators. In 2012 a study by the Royal Society, herbicide sprayed on GM-tolerant canola may have cut butterfly population by two-thirds and bee numbers in half.

In a 2009 comprehensive report, "Agriculture at the Crossroads" the question being, "Are GMO's necessary to feed the World?," found that modern biotechnologies will cause far more harm than helping subsistence farmers in developing countries. The problem is control by a relatively small number of multinational companies which can trigger significant social changes and adopt agricultural models that will not lead to poverty reduction nor sustainable practices. This will further increase dependency of local farmers on technological exports from wealthy countries.

Mike Adams, editor of *Natural News*, points out that gluten free foods most likely contain GMOs. This is due to the primary ingredient being corn which is 85% GMO, and has the Bt-toxin residue. When ingested, we run the risk of toxicity.

GMOs are still a radical agricultural experiment on the U.S. population at large. The only way to avoid GMO corn is to read labels and use USDA organic corn. Gluten free foods labeled ingredients as maltodextrin and corn syrup are GMO unless they are USDA organic. GMOs are banned in many countries of the world, while GMO labeling laws are prevalent as well in prominent countries of the world.

The FDA has approved Dow Chemicals' request to use *Enlist Duo*, a new dual insecticide combining 2,4-D (part of Agent Orange) with *glyphosate* from the USDA for soy and corn crops. This, despite the admission that 2,4-D usage will increase from 26 million pounds to 176 million pounds. 2,4-D is already the seventh largest source of dioxin in the U.S. It is already linked to birth defects, infertility, allergies, Parkinson's disease, endocrine disruption and cancer.

Dr. Gilles-Eric Seralini, professor of microbiology, University of Caen in France, published a peer-reviewed study of Monsanto's NK603 maize for long-term toxicity. They fed 200 rats either NK603 maize, glyphosate-treated (*Roundup*) or glyphosate in water for two years. There was evidence of liver and kidney toxicity in both groups, with a higher incidence of tumors. It was published in *Food & Chemical Toxicology* in November 2012 but retracted due to widespread criticism. The criticism was undeserved and the results of the study are frighteningly clear; glyphosate is hazardous. The rats were the same sample size and breed that Monsanto used in the 2004 study, but the Monsanto study was only for 90 days, which was not long enough to yield any adverse effects.

Research published by Dr. Johan Diels in December 2010 issue of *Food Policy* looked at "conflicts of interest" and how they affect biotech studies. His team at Portugese Catholic University analyzed 94 biotech papers, 100% of the *industryfunded* biotech scientists (41 out of 41) found no adverse effects from GMOs. Of the 51 that didn't have an industry scientist on the board, 12 found adverse effects. Dr. Michael K. Hansen, biologist and senior scientist at Consumers Union states that this is of "extreme high significance." We need peer-reviewed studies where there is no "conflict of interest."Tracy Fernandez Rysavy, editor in chief of Green America "would like the FDA to mandate independent, long-term testing of GMOs to ensure safety before turning them loose on the public. People should not have to be lab rats for the biotech industry."

## Peanuts update

An allergy update onpeanuts: Karen Kaplan in *Hamodia* (8-12-15) discussed the latest on peanut exposure. Dr. Anthony Fauci, the director of the National Institute on Allergy and Infectious Diseases

(NIAID) partially funded the study. The hygiene hypothesis states that we we live in a sanitized society, i.e, ultra clean and antiseptic with bacterial cleansers, which tend to lower immune function—creating more allergies and reducing resistance to germs. About 3% of the children in developed countries are now allergic to peanuts. In the UK children don't eat peanuts until one year old and in Israel, not until about 7 months old.

A systematic study was needed; so the Learning Early About Peanut Allergy (LEAPS) was created enrolling 640 infants. The study was led by Professor Gideon Lack at King's College, London. All were at risk for developing peanut allergy because of prior allergies to egg and/or a severe case of eczema. All infants were enrolled between 4 to 11 months of age. "There appears to be a narrow window of opportunity to prevent peanut allergy," says Dr. Lack. "As soon as infants develop the first signs of eczema or egg allergy in the first months of life, they should receive skin testing to peanut and then eat peanut products either at home if the test is negative or first under clinical supervision if the test if positive. Infants without such symptoms should be fed peanut products from four months of life."

A skin prick test was done to separate the reactors with no measurable wheal (a raised, red mark that itches) compared to reactors with a wheal of 1 to 4 mm in diameter into two groups. Primary outcome was assessed at 60 months of age.

Among the 530 infants with negative wheals, peanut allergy at 60 months was 13.7% and 1.9% in the consumption group. There was no significant difference in serious adverse events between groups.

Increase in Ig4 antibody primarily occurred in the consumption group; a greater percent of the avoidance group had elevated titers of Ig4 antibodies as well as a larger wheal.

Peanut exposure does have its side effects. There were 5 types—upper respiratory tract infections, viral skin infections, hives, gastroenteritis and conjunctivitis. These were more frequent among the peanuts eaters compared to avoiders. Side effects were either mild or moderate.

In summary the authors stated that the study was safe, tolerated, and highly efficacious. This study was published in the New England Journal of Medicine (NEJM, 2015 Feb 26;372(9): 806-13).The American Academy of Pediatrics has already withdrawn its endorsement of peanut avoidance and given the go-ahead to feed peanuts to young children. Researchers want to study further on how much peanut protein children actually have to eat to reduce their allergy risk, and if the protective effect wears off if they stop eating peanuts. The study will be titled LEAP-On.

## Some background on peanuts:

Peanuts are not a true nut but a legume or pea. Peanuts have a balanced amino acid content which is 20% protein and rich in nutrients. Their fat content is 75% and primarily unsaturated. Their B vitamin content is better than most nuts, because they are legumes. All B vitamins except B12 are present. Potassium, magnesium, and phosphorous are predominant minerals as well as zinc, copper, manganese, and iron.

## Aflatoxin caution:

Stored peanuts can be moldy, and trigger allergy to molds. The allergen is aflatoxin thought to be carcinogenic. In the United States, peanut butter should be selected without additives, otherwise it is frequently made with hydrogenated oil which makes it more toxic to the body. Other additives to avoid are salt, sugar and dextrose, rendering peanut butter a poor quality food.

## Specific Pollutants

Tina Beaudoin, N.D., in *Element*, #2, 2016, described the pervasiveness of toxic body burden in our society, in the *Fourth National Report on Environmental Chemicals of the CDC*. We have daily exposure to 108 of the 246 toxins (a small percent of the 1000's) present. They are classified as persistent and non-persistent types. Persistent Organic Pollutants (POPs) are cumulative with varying half lives. They include PCBs which are fat-soluble, and heavy metals, such as lead, cadmium and mercury. PCBs affect immune systems and organ functions, from thyroid to liver to cardiovascular.

They are in soil and water. PCBs in farmed salmon can have a half-life of 10-15 years in the body, while mercury in tuna can last 10-50 years. POPs are also in non-stick utensils which can cause reproductive, liver, and neurologic toxicity.

Non-persistent pollutants can include arsenic, herbicides, organophosphate and pyrethrine pesticides, solvents, polycyclic aromatic hydrocarbons, plastics and plasticizers and trihalomethane. The most important toxin in this group is arsenic, especially found in water from the United States to most countries including India, Pakistan and Afghanistan. Arsenic-containing feeds increase growth rate in animals to market sooner. Pork and poultry are especially high in arsenic to improve feed efficacy and growth and kill intestinal parasites.

Arsenic is a known cause of human diabetes, lung cancer in non-smokers, and a known carcinogen in general. Specifically it can lead to bladder cancer and other cancers as well as causing chemo-resistance to prostate cancer treatment. Arsenic can also block enzymes which help mineral absorption. Physiologically it can cause arrhythmia, coronary artery disease, stroke and peripheral vascular disease in high concentration. Arsenic-removing water filters are a necessity. Consider organic food consumption for meat, poultry and fruits and vegetables.

While bread is the staff of life, water is critical to survival. B. Dennis in "Don't Drink the Water," Hamodia, 6-22-2016, has emphasized that the EPA in two decades has not made regulations for contaminants in water that endanger public health. Only in 1990 did they almost set a standard for perchlorate—a chemical found in explosives, rocket fuel and road flares, and found in the drinking water supply of up to 16 million people.

Since 2013, Detlef Knapp and researchers at NC State University have identified high levels of 1,4-dioxane, a by-product of plastics, in waters along the Cape Fear river basin. The EPA states it as a "probable carcinogen." The EPA has a list of 100 unregulated contaminants in our water supplies from industrial sites and other sources. Their current inventory consists of two viruses and 28 chemicals, including 1,4-dioxane. The EPA is hampered by bureaucratic regulations and its slowness in review of toxic chemicals in our water. The EPA does, however, issue warnings of potentially toxic chemicals in our water—perfluorooctane sulfonate (PFOS) and perfluorooctanoic acid (PFOA).

Congress in June 2016, just passed a complete revision of the 1978 Toxic Substances Control Act for thousands of chemicals. The EPA can require health and safety data for untested chemicals before reaching the market and our drinking water. Implementation, though, may take years, and only if Congress funds it.

## Heavy Metal Toxicity—New Information

Note that thallium, a highly toxic heavy metal has been found in cruciferous vegetables such as kale, and is being studied by Dr. Rosenbaum and Ernest Hubbard. The toxicity of thallium rivals that of mercury and lead, and the three metals appear consecutively on the periodic table. In the January 2016 issue of the *Townsend Letter*, they reported on two pilot studies involving 40 and 50 people, respectively, one patient developing arrhythmia which disappeared when kale was removed from the diet. As in the first study, high thallium levels along with mercury and lead recurred in the second study.

With chronic thallium exposure, signs and symptoms include fatigue, headaches, depression, hallucinations, psychosis, dementia, poor appetite, leg pain, hair loss and vision disturbances. Chronic poisoning can occur within a matter of months to years through absorption of skin, respiratory or gastrointestinal tract where it can accumulate. It also mimics other diseases where it may be undetected.

## Thallium and Saddam Hussein:

Saddam Hussein would put thallium in bread and cakes which were fed to many people (see "Saddam kills enemies with slow poison," by Patrick Cockburn, January 31, 1995). The initial symptoms of thallium poisoning are primarily G.I. symptoms—nausea and vomiting and severe abdominal pain. The second to fifth day symptoms—nervous system effects with ascending neuropathy from the feet to the thighs, causing numbness, tingling, shooting pains and/or burning sensations in the skin. Progressive symptoms are lack of coordination, and ataxia which is common. Compared to other heavy metal poisoning, ataxia is predominant. Tremors and seizures can also take place. In addition to the brain and nervous system, it can affect the liver, kidneys, and heart. Thallium can displace potassium where it can interfere with major enzyme function—sodium potassium-ATPase which comprises 25% of the total energy in the body. It can bind to the ribosome of the mRNA of the cell which binds amino acids, and interfere with new proteins for healing, antibodies, and neurotransmitters. In Biochemistry, December, 2, 2008, 47 (48) entitled, "Thallium ions can replace both sodium and potassium ions in the glutamate transporter EAAC1," the result is, "correlated with some severe CNS disorders, such as amyotrophic lateral sclerosis (ALS, Lou Gehrig's disease), Huntington's disease, and Alzheimer's disease and the pathophysiology of brain insults (e.g., ischemia, hypoxia, hypoglycemia, epilepsy).

Due to the prevalence of toxins in our society as well as in most bodies of water such as London's Thames, toxins have been found in children as young as five years of age. Toxins especially *glyphosate*, a pesticide which has been in use since 1974, and which is distributed worldwide, can be inexpensively detected. Thetest uses a urine sample and costs $99.00 or $59.00 as part of an overall GPL-TOX PROFILE done by Great Plains Laboratory (see APPENDIX C). The cost of the complete GPL-TOX screen is $219.00 which includes 172 different environmental pollutants—including 2,4-D, part of *Agent Orange* in *Enlist* (Dow Chemical); also organophosphates used worldwide and phthalates used in plastics. One example is *Bisphenol A* (BPA) which is prevalent in fast foods and in processed foods. *Phthalates* are regulated in the EU but not in the U.S.

If you test positive for toxins, there are several steps to take:

1. *Eat organic foods as affordable.*
2. *Drink filtered water.*
3. *Switch to metal and glass containers instead of plastic water bottles and food containers.*
4. *Use infrared sauna to remove chemicals through sweating. This provides deep cleansing of the body.*
5. *Two supplements help the body detoxify. They are glutathione or its precursor, N-acetylcysteine.*
6. *Another supplement is niacin which can cause flushing. Use the lowest dose to start.*

## *Regenerative Agriculture*

## Need for agricultural change:

Agriculture is the foundation of civilization and a stable economy. When poorly practiced, it can be the most destructive industry.

The World Wildlife Fund postulates that since 1960, one third of the world's arable land will be gone through erosion and other degradation. Much of the deterioration is due to demand for GMO corn, soy, cotton, canola, sugar beet, and alfalfa crops. These are fed to farm animals to produce highly-subsidized, inefficient biofuels and processed foods. This cycle of planting mono-crops, and saturating the crops and fields with toxic chemicals depletes the soil nutrients, in particular—of minerals—and degrades the land, causing erosion.

## Reducing ecological stress with regenerative agriculture:

Overgrazing of pastures instead of managing livestock herds holistically, through managed, rotational grazing is equally destructive. It is important to restore ecological function as the only way to survive. This is implemented through "regenerative agriculture," reducing fossil fuel emissions, and reversing global deforestation. Alan Savory of the Savory Institute in London noted that regenerative agriculture represents a small minority, perhaps 3% to 5% of global agriculture. Unfortunately, 90% of the farmers, policy makers, and public still believe in the old agricultural model of chemistry, technology, and faulty policy. Savory further states that consumers need to be proactive and be aware that without agricultural change, we will have increasing poverty, hunger and global warming.

Richard Conniff, in the September 1, 2013 *Scientific American* article, "Microbes Help Grow Better Crops," discusses the use of bacteria and fungi which enrich soil as alternatives to pesticides and fertilizers which are increasingly less effective. Bacteria, fungi, and viruses naturally live in and around all plants—the microbiome. For example, West Coast tomatoes grow well in conjunction with bacteria that inhibit and kill *Salmonella*. The FDA has been experimenting with *Paenibacillus* spray on tomato seedlings that inhibit *Salmonella*. Since *Salmonella* and *E. coli* are common contaminants in foods, specific beneficial bacteria can protect the ground crops—

cantaloupes, spinach, sprouts, and other crops. There are as many as 40,000 microbe species in one gram of soil. This community labeled "agribiome" through low-cost DNA sequencing can be identified to be utilized in different seasons and soil environments to promote plant growth and minimize or eliminate pesticides and fertilizers. Note that increasing glyphosate use has produced super-resistant weeds, even with higher concentrations.

Sunflowers naturally produce a sugar called trehalose which stabilizes the plant membranes and protects the plant from seasons of dryness and rehydrates them. A Mexican molecular biologist, Gabriel Iturriaga, has identified a trehalose-producing bacteria, *Rhizobium etli*, that is found in the roots of bean plants. Their use can improve crop yields in general and provide relief under conditions of drought (see "The LEA proteins and trehalose loving couple: a step forward in anhydrobiotic engineering." *Biochemical Journal* Mar 01, 2008).

The agribiome has been known by farmers to naturally deliver fertile soil especially for soybeans, peanuts, and other legumes. The rhizobial—bacteria that live in nodules on their roots—are responsible by pulling nitrogen out of the air.

Phosphates are also required by plants. They are especially deficient in tropical soils. Phosphate fertilizers are not affordable for these nations. A solution is soil microbes, arbuscular mycorrhizal fungi which forms spores and filaments in and around the plant roots to provide phosphate. There are currently a few companies who produce the fungi in a culture and provide a concentrate as a gel. Cassava is a staple in developing countries which is being used to cut phosphate use in half and boost yields by 20%.

Agricultural symbiosis involves studying chemical signals that microbes use to communicate with each other. The object is to identify which bacteria are supplying plant nutrients or to find weaknesses in pathogens.

## Stress from sleep deprivation:

Sleep deprivation, according to Eve Van Cauter, director of the Sleep, Metabolism, and Health Center at the University of Chicago is a serious problem in this society. The body cannot accommodate sleep deficiency, and increases hunger and appetite. This only occurs in humans.

Specifically, when we do not get sufficient sleep:

- *Hormonal levels of the hunger hormone, ghrelin increase and decreased levels of the satiety hormone leptin occur. This can lead to overeating and weight gain.*

- *Calorie consumption can rise to 300 more calories than normal.*

- *We snack more and are less active.*

- *We eat more than needed to cover the energy cost of staying awake longer. This can lead to weight gain, especially being awake at night.*

- *Research has shown that less sleep for 5 days can lead to more carbohydrate consumption and up to 2 lbs. of weight gain.*

- *Lack of sleep activates the hypothalamic region in the brain and hormones affecting appetite regulation. Specifically, endocannabinoids are activated in the afternoon to stimulate eating for pleasure, called "hedonistic eating."*

- *There is reduced ability of the fat cells response to insulin for storage and utilization of energy. Insulin also promotes the secretion of leptin whereby fat cells are less sensitive, so weight gain ensues.*

Insulin and leptin contribute independently to fat intake or storage, according to senior researcher, Dr. Matthew Brady at the University of Chicago Medical School. As to sleep needs, Eve Van Cauter, PhD, states that young adults usually need seven to nine hours of sleep a night. As we age, fewer hours are needed—seven to eight hours are sufficient.

## DR. HERBERT I. SCHUCK

©Florie Freshman

## SOCIETAL STRESS

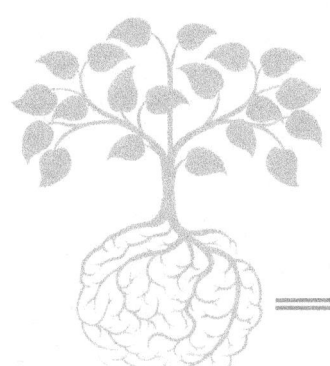

# Chapter 8

## Societal Stress

There is one more stressor that has been de-emphasized and even ignored. Dr. Herb, as a Naturopathic physician, with over twenty years experience, would like to focus on this—*societal stress*. Societal stress can manifest in symptoms beginning with depression/anxiety to end in suicide. Why? It seems to prevail in individuals who attain fame, e.g., movie stars, such as Robin Williams and others who struggle with substance abuse and/or alcohol, or who grow up amidst violence or inherit fortunes. Politicians, researchers and government officials when exposed to societal stress can also succumb to the pressure and become suicidal. Fame is difficult to cope with because of the perceived expectation to excel. We, as observers, hold these celebrities in high esteem until they crash with their own stressors in their attempts to overachieve. Societal pressures demand this, and even the elite and the rich may suffer from mental anguish and depression, just as we do, which can lead to suicide. Co-jointly, celebrities may also suffer from health problems—from heart disease to hypertension, to poor dietary habits.

## Suicides

Liz Szabo in *USA Today*, August 13, 2014, elaborates on this ignored problem facing Americans—we have twice as many suicides as homicides. Suicide kills more people than motor vehicle accidents—more then prostate cancer or leukemia. Suicides in the military have been increasing, especially in veterans between 18 to 29 years of age.

Gregg Zoroya in *USA Today*, July 7, 2016, notes that an average value of 20 veteran suicides per day in 2014, is based on current accurate statistics of males. This is four times the rate of active-duty service members.

David Shulkin, VA Undersecretary of Health, states that suicide rates among female veterans, 18 to 29, are more than double than that of non-serving woman.

The VA has taken several aggressive steps—adding more staff to the crisis hotline at 1-800-273-8255 to identify high risk veterans and adding more mental health counselors. VA Hospitals have group therapy but more individual therapy is limited to outside psychologists. But they need more in number to meet the demand.

Counseling, specifically with a psychologist who is certified to use cognitive behavioral therapy for anxiety and depression is useful for an individual, group, or on a couples basis. This works as well as antidepressants for mild to moderate depression. Stress as a problem by itself can also be dealt with by learning positive coping mechanisms through counseling. In addition, relearning responses to anxiety, anger and tension by promoting relaxation and calmness will buttress you from "overreacting." Trauma therapy for whatever the origin—from battleor from post-childhood abuse, accidents orbereavement (commonly known as PTSD), should be under the purview of the psychologist or group therapy leader to reduce stressful traumas and move toward positive solutions.

Congressman Tim Murphy, R-Pa, a child psychologist, introduced legislation to change the way mental illness is treated and funded. He states that in Robin Williams' age group, suicides have increased almost 30%. Murphy asked, "In what other discipline of medicine would we ignore such staggering statistics?"

Jonathan Rottenberg, Professor and psychologist at the University of Florida speaks of his own recovery from depression. He finds that younger people are more open to recognize mental illness as less of a moral stigma.

Dr. Elizabeth Minne, a psychologist from Austin, Texas commented on "All Things Considered" radio that suicide can be misinterpreted as an expression of liberation or freedom, "...that they might be [ wrongly] memorialized or viewed more positively." Dr. Minne explains that, "...suicide is never an option for working through distress—that there is always a way for us to get to a better place...I work to remind that person about all of the things that make that person special and valued—the things that I value in that individual. I work to connect them with other responsible people that can support him or her, including licensed professionals, suicide prevention hotlines and then I also encourage those people to engage in healthy activities that give them a *sense of joy*. Things that give them happiness."

In another article from *USA Today*, titled "If You Cure the Pain Do You Silence the Art?" it speaks about creativity and genius and expression through art. Kay Redfield Jamison, a professor at John Hopkins School of Medicine (who is also bipolar) speaks of the "tortured genius." She interviewed 50 writers and artists in Britain, and found that 38% had been treated for a mood disorder. Barry Panter, a psychiatrist and psychoanalyst, believes that art can be the external expression of internal emotional turmoil. Constance Scharff, director of Research at Cliffside, Malibu has treated celebrities with psychiatric issues and addiction. She believes that their creativity has come from their darkness, their agony, and their overindulgence in alcohol and drugs. Jeffrey Borenstein, president of Brain and Behavior Research Foundation in New York noted that ordinary people commit suicide every day—over 100 people. They all suffered from mental illness, and it was not a matter of high or low intelligence.

There are many success stories in recovery from depression.

J.K. Rowling had depression and suicidal thoughts in her struggle as a single mother. She of course went on to write the *Harry Potter* novels. Winston Churchill, Vincent Van Gogh, and Abraham Lincoln (including his wife) also had to battle depression and succeeded.

Dr. Nancy C. Andreasen, Chair of Psychiatry at the University of Iowa, has been examining the creative brain through neuroimaging. She states that most of the individuals interviewed feel that *treatment enhances their creativity*. She comments that Jonathan Winters, Robin Williams' mentor, was also bipolar.

With the death of the beloved Robin Williams, it has spurred an increase in crisis hotlines and mental illness volunteering. The *National Suicide Prevention Center* at 1-800-273-8255 especially has seen higher volumes of calls. John Draper, PhD, the project director of the lifeline noted that the national center receives only 12% of the calls, while the rest connect with 160 local crisis centers across the country. He states there is increased awareness of people in distress. Calls to the *National Alliance on Mental Illness (NAMI)* 1-800-950-6264 have resulted in more volunteering. There is also a "speak out" tab on the website.

Paul Holtzheimer, director of mood disorders service at Dartmouth Geisel School of Medicine emphasized the need for responsible media coverage rather than sensational which is harmful. Proper coverage can increase awareness of depression and the benefits, leading people to get help.

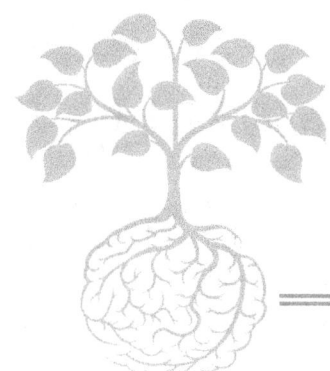

# Chapter 9

## *Lifestyle Changes*

More involved lifestyle changes can benefit the individual in a permanent way, such as remodeling your house, which takes some thought and planning but increases home value in the long term. Personal changes can pay dividends for improving overall health through reducing blood pressure, decreasing cardiac risk for stroke and heart attack, and losing weight. These changes will improve quality of life and enjoyment of longevity.

Additional lifestyle changes may include meditation, yoga, exercise, massage, counseling, sauna, classes on stress reduction, cognitive behavioral counseling (CBT), mindfulness practice, debt refinancing, dealing with past traumas, and other considerations structured to one's individual needs.

### New Choices Wanted For Retirees

A new survey, by *Life Re-imagined* and *USA Today* was done of pre-retirees, ages 40 to 59 years of age about future plans to reduce stress in our society. Plans included a major career shift to give back to society. Those people wanted more balance in life, increased flexibilty, and ability to learn. Emilio Pardo, AARP Executive Vice President and President of Life Re-imagined (https://lifereimagined.aarp.org) states that midlife may be a good time for a career shift.

Marci Alboher, Vice President of Marketing and Communications at Encore.org and one of the nation's leading authorities on career issues and workplace trends, states that older Americans want more meaningful lives and to provide a legacy. The survey also shows that over half of pre-retirees would quit their job tomorrow if money was not a problem. Desired changes in the next 5 to 10 years for older adults included giving back to society, pursuing their passions, traveling, learning a new hobby or changing their personal or professional lives.

Bloomfield and Cooper promote recognition of some mind/body distress signs:

- *Time Urgency*
- *Tension—usually with muscle tightness*
- *Tiredness*
- *Mistakes*
- *Irritability*
- *Distractions—Lack of focus, concentration, forgetfulness.*
- *Hunger or Thirst*
- *Feeling Blue*
- *Aggression or Hostility*

LIFESTYLE CHANGES

MEDITATE TWICE DAILY

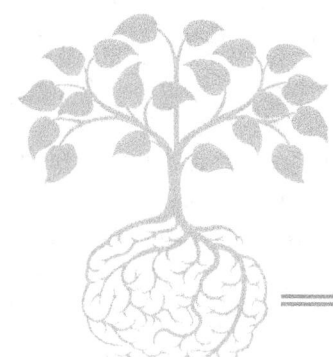

# Chapter 10

## *Meditation, Cognitive Behavioral Therapy and Mindfulness*

Let us now detail some specific changes:
M. Ricard, A. Lutz, and R.J. Davidson discussed in the "Mind of the Meditator," progress in contemplative practices which benefit both body and mind. Advances in neuroimaging and other technologies have provided insight in brain function during three major types of Buddhist meditation—focused attention, mindfulness, compassion and lovingkindness.

In *Focused Attention Meditation,* the meditator concentrates on the in-and-out cycle of breathing. This stimulates the posterior cingulate cortex, the precuneus and other areas to prevent inattention.

In *Mindfulness or Open-Monitoring Meditation,* there is observing sights, sounds, and other sensations inclusive of internal body sensations and thoughts.

In *Compassion and Lovingkindness Meditation,* the meditator fosters benevolence towards others—including friends and enemies. The temporoparietal junction shows increased activity.

The researchers also found that long-term Buddhist practitioners sustained a particular EEG pattern, called highamplitute gamma-band oscillations and phase synchrony at 25 and 42 hertz. These oscillations can integrate cognitive and affective functions during learning and conscious perception. This can affect lasting changes in brain circuitry.

S.W. Lazar from Harvard University and colleagues studied long-time meditators and a control group, finding that the volume of the brain's darker tissue, the gray matter differed in the prefrontal and insula cortices—specifically Brodmann areas 9 and 10, which are frequently stimulated during meditation. Differences were were prominent in older meditators. Lazar and colleagues in a follow-up study noted that mindfulness training deceased the volume of the amygdala, involved in fear processing for participants and reduced stress over time.

Author Dawn Groves suggests meditation for five-minutes for busy people and Sarah McLean who teaches meditation in Sedona, Arizona suggests meditation for up to twenty minutes for more effective results.

Exercises include preparatory deep breathing, guided body relaxation from head to toe; followed by the meditation itself. Eyes are closed and awakening is done gradually at the end. Posture ranges from sitting at a desk at work or on a chair at home or Yogi style sitting on a cushion in a group.

Dawn Groves in her book, *Meditation for busy people: 60 seconds to serenity*, reviews specifics. Meditation improves both body and mind: The body is helped by reducing blood pressure and relaxing muscles; the mind is helped by teaching compassion and tolerance for others and increasing awareness of thoughts and feelings before you act on them.

It can also improve stamina for busy lifestyles. Before meditating, you need to be sitting and use good body posture with a straight back and head held high.

The basic steps of meditation are:

1. *Relaxation, whereby muscles can reduce tension beginning with focus on your feet progressively moving up the body to legs, hips, abdomen, shoulders and arms, neck and head.*
2. *Center, where the focus is on deep diaphragmatic breathing or mindfulness, i.e., grounding yourself to only listen to the quiet and peacefulness of your body. Creative visualization is a method to picture certain pleasurable experiences or goals to achieve which are joyous and peaceful.*
3. *Release is the "cool down" or shift from mental consciousness to your body. Initially, you move your fingers and toes progressively, stretching to the head and neck and arms. Gradually you open your eyes to be aware of your surroundings.*
4. *Do an honest appraisal of what you gained and keep a diary to reinforce these positive experiences.*

Meditation times can vary from a minimum of five minutes to fifteen minutes or longer. You can be alone or in a group; have music which is soft and gentle. Anything else to enhance the experience—incense or candles are suitable. If you are restless, focus on your breathing or change body posture or note where in your body is this feeling. Lastly if it is worry and anxiety in your thoughts, recognize it, and speak it out loud—for example, "I'm feeling uptight in my gut." Most importantly, schedule a regular time of day for meditation—both in the morning and evening. Look forward with apositive expectancy to your experience. Sarah McLean encourages participants to visualize, "I am thankful for..." prior to each session.

Dr. Tina Beaudoin describes another type of meditation called Transcendental Meditation or TM in which an individual in the lotus position relaxes and chants a word, phrase, prayer or sound, such as "OM" repeatedly. Other choices she mentions include:

heart-centered concentration, reflective mindfulness and creative meditation. Dr. Beaudoin notes the benefits for health and wellness—reducing anxiety and relieving depression, maintaining focus, and reducing negative stimuli.

Dr. Herb did a one-day session on Cognitive Behavioral Therapy (CBT) given by Daniel J. Moran, PhD., the founder of the Midamerican Psychological Institute, a psychotherapy clinic in south Chicago. Dr. Moran coauthored the books ACT in Practice and Evidence-Based Education Methods. CBT can be applied to treat depression, anxiety, anger, eating disorders, trauma, and PTSD.

The six basic principles are:

1. *Cognition is the most important determinant of human emotion.*
2. *Dysfunctional thinking is a major determinant of emotional distress.*
3. *The best way to conquer distress is to change this thinking.*
4. *Multiple factors precede irrational thinking.*
5. *Emphasis is on the present rather then historical influences of behavior.*
6. *Irrational beliefs can be changed into rational beliefs.*

Albert Ellis was the founder of CBT. His three-day seminars continue to be given in New York on weekends. The goal is to replace irrational beliefs—anger, depression, guilt, and anxiety with rational beliefs—specifically clinically relevant behaviors, reinforcement of proper behaviors, and generalization of those behaviors to other settings.

Beyond CBT, there is a further development of Acceptance and Commitment Therapy (ACT) by Daniel J. Moran. This is built on empirically-based principles to increase psychological flexibility with a mindfulness component and behavioral change strategies. In this manner, stress-related disorders can be treated as well as smoking addictions, various other addictions, pain, PTSD, anxiety, and depression.

Mindfulness is another method of stress reduction espoused and developed by Jon Kabat-Zinn, Professor of Medicine emeritus, and the founding director of The Stress Reduction Clinic and the Center for Mindfulness in Medicine, Health Care, and Society at the University of Massachusetts Medical School. He leads workshops on stress reduction and mindfulness for physicians and other health professionals and lay audiences worldwide. His most well-known book, *Wherever You Go There You Are*, provides a simple path to incorporate mindfulness into one's own life.

Mindfulness-based stress reduction (MBSR) is a well-defined, systematic approach to self-care that is participatory and based on mindfulness meditation. It is an evidence-based treatment approach for emotional and physical conditions. It is conducted in a supportive, non-judgmental environment which emphasizes self-efficacy and self-reliance. The full course is a 31 hour, heterogenous model. Dr. Herb completed a one-day course on Mindfulness Based Stress Reduction by Elana Rosenbaum, MS, LICSW, normally a three-day intensive course. Elana personally trained under Jon Kabat-Zinn.

Neuroscience on mindfulness has shown support for the prefrontal cortex which promotes a sense of well-being and approach (vs avoidance) as well as growth of the hippocampal gray matter. Perceived stress increases the gray matter in the amygdala while mindfulness decreases it (threat reduction).

Mindfulness provides intention and commitment, focus and attention on the moment: thoughts and feelings, and where thoughts and feelings are experienced in the body. It teaches to be aware of one's breathing. Mindfulness meditation can be done sitting, walking, or yoga style. When doing this meditation, be aware of your attitude and its effect on the body. Note your stressors and how you cope. Communicate. With this method, you can practice up to forty-five minutes a day.

Massage is another technique promoting relaxation. It soothes the soul—it releases tension throughout the body by relaxing the musculature. Again seek a licensed massage therapist (LMT) who may offer specific techniques— Swedish, Shiatsu, Rolfing, and others.

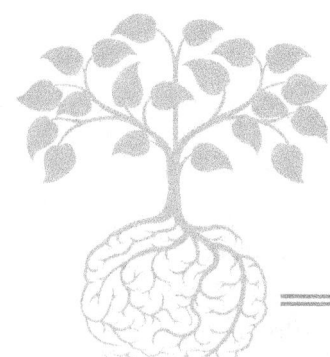

# Chapter 11

## Creative Modalities—Art, Music

**Art therapy:**

Barbara Becker at Art 4 Fun (http://www.art4funstudio.com) in Phoenix, Arizona has promoted art therapy for over seventeen years. Art therapy is a forgotten method of stress relief from which children as young as six years of age to retired adults can benefit.

**Modalities offered are:**

- Glass fusing which is fired in a kiln twice for colors and shapes.
- Painting on silk—described as mesmerizing.
- Acrylic painting on canvas which can include mixed media.
- Watercolor painting on illustration board or watercolor paper.

- *Clay—hand building.*
- *Hot Glass mosaics.*

## Music therapy:

Music therapy is a modality often overlooked since it is prevalent in all places as "piped-in" music, both outdoors and indoors. It is also predominant as "noise" when overly loud, such as in some rapper-style music or that which is blaring out of someone's home or car window. This noise creates disturbance rather than calm in people. To reduce stress, music should be enjoyable and soothing. Music therapy is an allied health profession within a therapeutic relationship that can address the physical, psychological, cognitive and social needs of individuals.

The American Music Therapy Association, (http://www.musictherapy.org) defines Music Therapy as the clinical and evidence-based use of music interventions to accomplish individualized goals within a therapeutic relationship by an accredited professional who has completed an approved music therapy program.

## Music therapy interventions can:

- *Promote Wellness*
- *Manage Stress*
- *Alleviate Pain*
- *Express Feelings*
- *Enhance Memory*
- *Improve Communication*
- *Promote Physical Rehabilitation*

Music therapy has been successful in children and adolescents with autism as well as in schizophrenia and dementia. Treatments included both passive listening to music and active participation in the singing of popular songs with other patients (see the British Journal of Psychiatry Supplement, Aug 1994;(24):38-44, PMID: 7946230)

## Physical skills therapy:

Physical skills, such as movement and agility can improve individual and group socialization in their environment. Communication for families can also be facilitated with improved physical skills. The benefits of improved physical skills can be utilized—by cancer patients, attention-deficit children, veterans, depressed and/or anxious individuals, for pain management, reduction of muscle tension and for disabled children. Physical skills use for dementia and hospice care is also being explored.

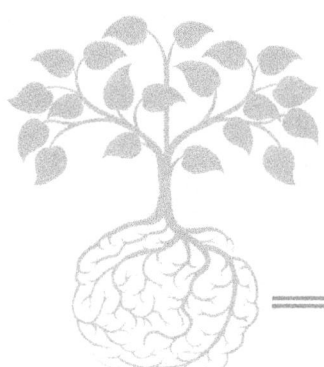

# Conclusion

In summary, Dr. Herb has become aware of the complex influence of stress on the human physiology—from fertilization of the embryo, to the mother's attitude during pregnancy, to the birthing process and the health of the child, to society's openness to the event. The most important aspect however, is the mental and emotional ennui of the mother and the child, and the interaction of the family and our society.

In our overly fast-paced society, in the Digital Age, we can move too quickly and ignore "the forest for the trees." Rather, we should center or ground ourselves, and set aside at least ten minutes to one hour twice daily to meditate, pray, relax, breathe and be grateful for life.

*Herbert I. Schuck, N.D., M.Sc. Pharm.*

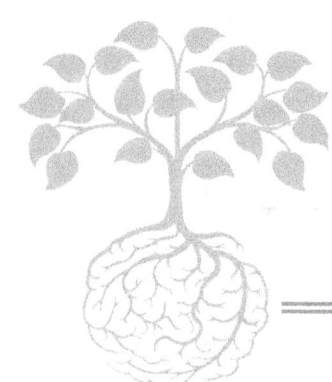

# Appendix A

| LAB ANALYSIS | ZRT | LABRIX | NEUROSCIENCE | DIAGNOSTECHS |
|---|---|---|---|---|
|  | No NT | NT – NJ.,CT.,MA., Sweden, Not in NY. |  | Not offered |
| Urine | Elements: $I_2$, Se,Br,Hg,As |  | NY with outside NY address | No |
| Blood spot | Cardiometabolic Thyroid Vitamin D No blood spot in NY | No blood spot |  | No |
| Urine | Female hormones Sex hormones |  |  | No |
| Saliva | Saliva OK | Need Clinician | Adrenals Sex hormones | Saliva OK Adrenals Sex hormones Female hormones |
| Serum [1] Blood MELISA | No | No | Thyroid Cytokines $I_2$ | Not offered |

| Providers Authorized | Compounding pharmacy M.D., D.O., N.D., N.P. Need to write Rx | Nutritionist Health food stores N.P.,N.D.,LAc, M.D., D.O., pharmacy, Dentists | Pharmacist, M.D., D.O., N.P., N.D. | Health care providers |
|---|---|---|---|---|
| Key: NT = neurotransmitters | | | | |

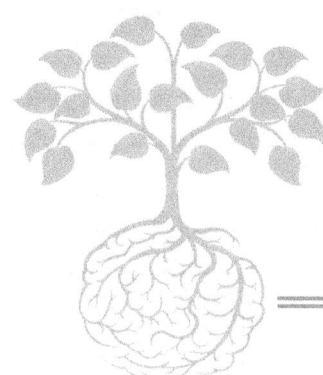

# Appendix B

Neurotransmitters are of two types:

1. *Excitatory—stimulate brain and body*
2. *Inhibitory—calm brain and body*

| EXCITATORY NEUROTRANSMITTERS | | | | |
|---|---|---|---|---|
| **TYPE** | **IMPORTANT FOR** | **HIGH LEVELS** | **LOW LEVELS** |
| Aspartic Acid | Vital for energy and brain function | Seizures Anxiousness | Tiredness Low mood |
| Epinephrine | Motivation, Energy, Mental focus | Sleep difficulties Anxiousness Attention issues | Fatigue Lack of focus Difficult weight loss |
| Norepinephrine | Mental focus Emotional stability | Anxiousness Stress Hyperactivity High blood Pressure | Lack of energy Lack of focus Lack of motivation Low mood |
| Dopamine | Feelings of pleasure and satisfaction, Muscle control and function | Poor Intestinal function Developmental delay Attention issues | Addictions Cravings |

| | | | |
|---|---|---|---|
| Glutamate | Primary NT for learning and memory | Anxiousness Low mood Seizures Psychological and immunological symptoms | Tiredness Poor brain activity |
| Phenylethylamine (PEA) | Focus and concentration | Mind racing Sleep difficulties Anxiousness | Difficulty paying attention Difficulty thinking clearly Low mood |
| Histamine | Controls sleep-wake cycle; energy and motivation | Allergic responses Sleep difficulties | Feeling tired |

| Inhibitory Neurotransmitters | | | |
|---|---|---|---|
| TYPE | IMPORTANT FOR | HIGH LEVELS | LOW LEVELS |
| Gamma amino butyric acid (GABA) | Primary NT in brain and calmness and relaxation | Hyperactivity Anxiousness Sleep difficulties | Severe Hyperactivity Severe Anxiousness Severe Sleep difficulties |
| Glycine | Like GABA—calmness and relaxation | Anxiousness Low mood Stress-related dissorders | No associated clinical symptoms to date |
| Taurine | Proper heart function, healthy sleep, and calmness | Hyperactivity Anxiousness Sleep difficulties | Severe Hyperactivity Severe Anxiousness Severe Sleep difficulties |
| Serotonin | Mood, sleep, and appetite | SSRI medications | Low mood Sleep difficulties Uncontrolled appetite Headaches Hot Flashes |

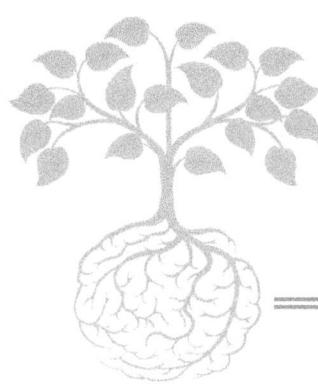

# Appendix C

Zrt Lab Llc
866-600-1636
Beaverton, OR 97008
www.zrtlab.com

Labrix Clinical Services Inc.
16256 Se 130 Ave.
Clackamus, OR 97015
503-342-8069
www.labrix.com

Neuroscience 373 280 St.
Osceola, WI 54020
888-342-7272
www.neuroscienceinc.com

Diagnostechs, Inc.
800-878-37877
6620 S. 192 Pl., J106
Kent, Wa 98032
www.diagnostechs.com

Great Plains Laboratory, Inc
11813 W. 77 St.
Lenexa, Ks 66214
913-341-8949
www.greatplainslaboratory.
com

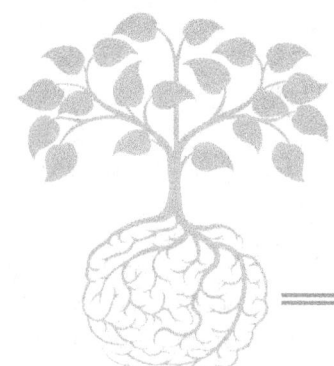

# References

*Mind Matters,* Millenson, J.R., PhD, MRH 1995

*Transforming Anxiety,* Childre Doc and Deborah Rozman, 2006. New Harbinger Publications, Inc. Oakland, CA 94609

*They Can't Find Anything Wrong,* Clarke, David D. 2007. Sentient Publications, Boulder, CO 80302

*Understanding Healthcare and Stress Management,* Mark Percival, D.C., N.D., 1991

*Stress Less,* Thea Singer, 2010

*Mind as Healer, Mind as Slayer,* Kenneth R. Pelletier 1977

*The Stress of Organizational Change,* "Survival Guide," Price Pritchett and Ron Pound

*The Power of 5,* Bloomfield, Harold H. and Cooper, Robert K., 1995

*Meditation for Busy People,* Grover, Dawn, 1993 USA Today-2014 to 2016. Numerous articles

Green America January/February 2014—*GMOs and the Case for Precaution*

Hamodia, 2014 to 2016. Several articles

Scientific American—the Food Issue: September 2013

Haas, Elson M., *Staying Healthy with Nutrition* REV. 1992, p. 337

Hass, Elson, M.D. and Levin, Buck, Phd, *Staying Healthy With Nutrition,* 2006

Karen Kaplan, *New Study To Fight Peanut Allergies, Eat Peanuts*, Hamodia, 8-12-2015

Focus, December 2015, *The Golden Age of Gluten Free Living: New Findings, Test, and Treatments.*

Practice Points: *State of the Art Diagnostic Workup of Gluten Spectrum Disorders*, Born, Todd A. (GSD)

Barbara Becker, Art for Fun, Phoenix, AZ 85014

2013 Report by Cleveland Clinic, "Problem Foods: Is It Allergy or Intolerance," Dargon, Christine, Ph.D.,*Anxiety Disorders In Children & Adolescents*

M. Ricard, A. Lutz, R.J. Davidson, Scientific American, *The Neuroscience of Meditation*, November 2014

Neuroscience—Neurotransmitters 101—*A Guide to Understanding the Role of the Nervous System in Health* Lu,T.K. and Purcell, O, Machine Life, Scientific American, April 2016

Y. Tusk, M.Sc, Hamodia, July 6, 2016, *Breakfast—The Most Important Meal of the Day*

GPL-TOX : *Toxic Non-Metal Chemical Profile*, Great Plains Laboratory.

Dr. Sherry Rogers, Total Wellness, November 2007, *Arsenic Unavoidable, So We Must Get Rid of It*

J. Castle, *Nutrients to Combat the Modern Stress Epidemic*, Life Extension, Jan/Feb. 2012

Holistic Primary Care, *Are FODMAPS the New GLUTEN?* Sept. 24, 2013

*Do You Have SIBO?*, Josh Axe, M.D.

*The IBS Within the IBD*, Gary Weiner, NDNR, Jan 2016.

*What Do We Really Know About Roundup Weed Killer?* by Elizabeth Grossman, National Geographic, April 23, 2015 (http://news.nationalgeographic. com/2015/04/150422- glyphosate-roundup-herbicide-weeds).

*Monsanto's Preharvest Staging Guide use of Roundup* (http:// roundup.ca/_uploads/documents/MON-Preharvest%20 Staging%20 Guide.pdf).

*New Analysis of a Rat Feeding Study with a Genetically Modified Maize Reveals Signs of Hepatorenal Toxicity.* Séralini, GE., Cellier, D. & de Vendomois, J.S. Arch Environ Contam Toxicol (2007) 52: 596. doi:10.1007/s00244-006-0149-5.

FEBS Lett. 2000 Sep 15;481(2):164-8. *DNA stability in plant tissues: implications for the possible transfer of genes from genetically modified food.* Chiter A, Forbes JM, Blair GE. School of Biochemistry and Molecular Biology, Room 8.10a Garstang Building, University of Leeds, Mount Preston Street, Leeds, UK.

"RPAH Elimination Diet Handbook," 2009, Anne Swain, Velencia Soutter, Robert Loblay, Allergy Unit, Royal Prince Alfred Hospital. (http://emerge.org.au/wp-content/ uploads/2014/11/RPAH-Elimination-Diet-Handbookwith-food-shopping-guide.pdf)

Sapolsky, RM, et al, "Neuroendocrinology of Aging" *Endocrine Reviews*, 1986, Vol 7, pp 284-301

Sorrels, S.F., et al, "The Stressed CNS When Glucocorticoids Aggravate Inflammation"

www.ingramcontent.com/pod-product-compliance
Lightning Source LLC
LaVergne TN
LVHW011720060526
838200LV00051B/2974